Sweet F.A.

A Play with Songs

Written by
Tim Barrow and Paul Beeson

Dramaturgy by
Bruce Strachan

TIPPERMUIR
· BOOKS LIMITED ·

This first edition published and copyright 2022 by Tippermuir Books Ltd, Perth, Scotland. mail@tippermuirbooks.co.uk – www.tippermuirbooks.co.uk.

ISBN 978-1-913836-14-6 (paperback)

A CIP catalogue record for this book is available from the British Library.

Editorial and Project coordination by Dr Paul S Philippou.

Cover design by Matthew Mackie. Cover photograph: Simon Messer. Editorial support: Alan Laing, Steve Zajda.

Text styling, layout, and artwork by Bernard Chandler [graffik]. Text set in Interstate Light 9/11.5pt with Bold titling.

Printed and bound by Ashford Colour Press Ltd, Gosport PO13 0FW

To Daisy, Jessie and Zoa

SWEET F.A. CAST

THE TEAM

RENÉE (REENIE) BROWN

HARRIET (HARRY) HARPER

MAUREEN (MO) JARDINE

HELEN MATTHEWS

ALICE McEWAN

LILY (LIL) McKENZIE

DAISY ROBERTSON

THE S.F.A.

ABERCROMBIE

BUCHANAN

CAMPBELL

LORD DUNDEE

LORD SCUNTHORPE

SECRETARY WATT

OTHERS

ANN
ROSIE } ENSEMBLE AND MUSICIANS/SINGERS

FOUR MEN

ALFRED FRANKLAND

THREE SOLDIERS

SWEET F.A.

'We are thrilled to be returning to Tynecastle Park with a brand new production, telling this timely tale of the rise of women's football during the First World War. After an uncertain, disrupted time it feels more vital than ever to bring people together to tell stories. We're grateful to Hearts for allowing us to take advantage of the outdoor, covered facilities in the main stand at Tynecastle, and we immensely look forward to meeting Tynecastle audiences again, telling this important story about women's football – including its historical connection to the ground. We vividly remember the brilliant reception they gave *A War of Two Halves* and they, and new audiences, can expect a similar blend of history, humour, passion and poignancy from this brilliant tale.'

Bruce Strachan, *Director*

'We're delighted to be able to welcome back the team from This is My Story Productions with a brand new story to tell. The resurgence of women's football in the early twentieth century, to huge popularity, and the subsequent barriers and bans by authorities had a huge and lasting impact. *Sweet F.A.* manages to brilliantly capture the spirit of those war years and deliver a little bit of history with some real laugh-out-loud moments. Something I think we're all in need of just now.'

Lianne Parry, *Head of Heritage,*
Heart of Midlothian Football Club

'Bruce Strachan's production is sharp, funny and well-drilled...the cast have the coordination and sparkle of Premier League champions.'

Mark Fisher, *The Guardian*

'*Sweet F.A.* Is a charming piece of educational theatre from an all-female cast... *Sweet F.A.* is testament to what can happen if the world of sports and the arts come together.'

Francesca Lynn, *The Indiependent*

'This is full-throated theatre, as straightforward in its message and appeal as a football chant (one of the family-friendly ones, of course).'

Alice Saville, *The Financial Times*

'Moving and well-balanced historical play with songs combines popular appeal with social relevance.'

Thom Dibdin, *The Stage*

''Through the absolute specifics and detail in this piece, they achieve a story that has a universality that could be recognised by all – a rare blend.'

Fiona Orr, *Musical Theatre Review*

'A remarkable and thoroughly enjoyable tale of women's football, and its strange rollercoaster history.'

Joyce McMillan, *The Scotsman*

'Ballsy brilliant production celebrating football and female emancipation.'

Claire Wood, *The Wee Review*

'*Sweet F.A.* is a rumbustious thing, full of humour and pawky abandon... In intent and execution, this has to be counted as a roaring success.'

Hugh Simpson, AllEdinburghTheatre.com

ORIGINAL CAST AND PRODUCTION TEAM

Tynecastle Park, 5-30 August 2021

Helen Matthews/Alfred Frankland	Heather Cochrane
Rosie/Campbell/Soldier 2/Man 2	Jodie Differ
Maureen (Mo) Jardine/Abercrombie/Man 3	
	Laura Harvey
Lily (Lil) McKenzie//Secretary Watt	Heather Horsman
Ann/Buchanan/Soldier 1/Man 4	Rachel Macpherson-Graham
Daisy Robertson/Campbell	Ria McLeod
Alice McEwan/Soldier 3	Rachel Millar
Harriet (Harry) Harper/Lord Dundee/Man 1	
	Lucy Pedersen
Renée (Reenie) Brown/Lord Scunthorpe	
	Elspeth Turner
Director	Bruce Strachan
Writers	Paul Beeson and Tim Barrow
Composer and Musical Director	Matthew Brown
Movement Director	Stephanie Arsoska
Sound Designer and Show Op	Ian Cunningham
Set Designer	Eve Murray
Costume Designer	Natasha Murray
Costume Assistant	Keira Dunnet
Associate Producer	Simon Beattie

The following people/organisations were involved in supporting the production:

Lianne Parry, David Stevenson, Sarah Pulley and Queen Margaret University, Jo Barrow and The Edinburgh Makars,

Sheelagh Strachan and Moira Newby, Ann Park, the Control Room and staff at HMFC, Dundee & Angus College.

Special thanks to Brendan Cantwell and ASC Scaffolding for their extremely generous sponsorship of the production.

This Is My Story Productions was formed in 2017 to stage *A War of Two Halves*, which played to rave reviews and fantastic audience acclaim at Tynecastle Park as part of the Edinburgh Fringe in 2018 and 2019. Nonsense Room Productions was established in 2002.

Their previous shows at the Edinburgh Fringe include: *The Ballad of James II* by Douglas Maxwell, *A Midsummer Night's Dream*, *Romeo and Juliet*, *The Apprentice* by Simon Beattie, and *Handling Bach* by Paul Barz, all performed at the iconic Rosslyn Chapel.

All live music performed by Jodie Differ and Elspeth Turner.

Its work for young people includes: *Hairy Maclary & Friends*, *Shark in the Park*, *You Choose* and *Little Red Riding Hood*.
In 2011, *Hairy Maclary & Friends* was invited to play at Sydney Opera House, Australia, for its Christmas season. Since then it has been invited to take part in the acclaimed Kidsfest in both Hong Kong and Singapore, and has toured extensively in the UK, Ireland, Australia and New Zealand.

www.thisismystoryproductions.co.uk

Also Available

A War of Two Halves is the debut show from This Is My Story Productions, written by Paul Beeson and Tim Barrow, and directed by Bruce Strachan. It tells the famous tale of the 1914 Heart of Midlothian football team who, on the verge of winning the league, volunteered en masse to fight in France in the First World War with McCrae's Battalion.

ABOUT THE AUTHORS

Tim Barrow is the co-writer of *Sweet F.A.* He trained as an actor at Drama Centre London, graduating with a BA Hons in 2001. His debut play, *Guy*, played at London's Pleasance Theatre, directed by Michael Fentiman. *Union* premiered at Edinburgh's Lyceum Theatre, directed by Mark Thomson, and is published by Playdead Press. *Neither God Nor Angel* played at Oran Mor/Traverse, directed by Ryan Alexander Dewar. Tim was one of five writers who created *The Sunnyside Centre* for Village Pub Theatre, directed by Caitlin Skinner. *A War Of Two Halves,* co-written with Paul Beeson, played at Tynecastle Park in 2018 and 2019. Tim founded Lyre Productions to make independent Scottish feature films, writing and producing the award-winning indie Scottish road movie *The Inheritance*, Edinburgh love story *The Space Between*, and schizophrenia love story road movie *Riptide* – currently screening at film festivals worldwide.

Paul Beeson is the co-writer of *Sweet F.A.* He is an Edinburgh-born actor, writer, teacher and co-founder of This Is My Story Productions. He has many theatre credits and has previously toured the UK and internationally with acclaimed company Nonsense Room Productions, performing in shows including *Shark in the Park*, *You Choose!* and *Ae Fond Kiss*. Paul's first venture into writing was sketch show *A Beginner's Guide to the Fringe* in 2005 after which he co-wrote and performed in the critically successful Edinburgh Fringe sell-out production *A War of Two Halves* in 2018 and 2019. The play received 5-star reviews and was one of BritishTheatre.com's Critics Choices of 2019. He has also co-written three short films: *The Hardest Hobbit to Break*, *Route de Sort* and *Last Night in the Cockpit.* He is currently developing two comedy drama series, *The VHS Diaries* and *Theatre in Education*, and has also recently filmed a pilot for Scottish sitcom *Game of Cones* and recorded an audio drama called *From An Island.*

Bruce Strachan is the director of *Sweet F.A.* He trained at the Royal Scottish Academy of Music and Drama (now RCS). He works as an acting teacher, director and producer, and is currently a lecturer in acting at Queen Margaret University, Edinburgh. He has worked throughout the UK for companies including Hull Truck, TAG Theatre Glasgow, The Arches, The National Youth Theatre of Great Britain and the National Theatre of Scotland. Bruce has been artistic director of Nonsense Room Productions since 2002 and has directed many shows including *Shark in the Park*, *You Choose!* as well as *Hairy Maclary & Friends* in both the UK and internationally – including a summer season at Sydney Opera House. For This Is My Story Productions, he directed and co-produced *A War of Two Halves* – the story of the legendary 1914-15 Hearts football team – first performed at Tynecastle Park in 2018.

DIRECTOR'S NOTE

This play was intended to be performed initially at Tynecastle Park with a view to it being able to be performed in any stadium, given the broad relevance of the subject matter. As creators, we are open to the notion of it being relocated to any city or town where it can work. Adapting the piece to work in a different location would be permissible provided the core sentiments of the piece are maintained. Please contact us (using the email address below) if you would like any guidance in this regard. In addition, the play will work as a traditional theatre piece too, or indeed as a promenade production which was our original intention for *Sweet F.A.*

The play was written against a backdrop of significant upheaval for Heart of Midlothian Football Club and the Scottish Premier Football League. There are jokes and references to this period that will no doubt lose their relevance and significance over time, although football fans have notoriously long memories for injustices; feel free to update or remove these references as you see fit.

The songs are a vital component of the piece and contain some of the most powerful moments of drama. There is a fine score available for the piece, composed by Matthew Brown, which will be made available along with rights.

www.thisismystoryproductions.co.uk
thisismystoryproductions@gmail.com

FOREWORD

Sweet F.A. began life in August 2018 with a conversation between myself and Ann Park (Director - Communities and Partnerships at Heart of Midlothian Football Club). Whilst discussing ideas for a follow-up piece to *A War of Two Halves*, we talked about other key historical periods and events that are part of the fascinating history of the club. Ann pointed out that 2021 was the anniversary of the 1921 ban on women's football. Just before this ban came into effect there had been a women's match at Tynecastle Park which had drawn a big crowd and had been refereed by one of Hearts' legendary players, Bobby Walker.

I was struck by how little I knew about this and was intrigued to learn more. The notion of a 'sister piece' to *A War of Two Halves*, with women at the heart of the story, was hugely appealing. Paul, Tim and I set out to research the early days of the women's game, and were fascinated and shocked both by what we found and what we didn't find. We discovered there was very little detailed research available at all on Scottish women's football, indeed verified details of that particular Tynecastle match are sparse.

This contrast between the known facts, indicating the clear scale and popularity of a game attracting 53,000 for one match in 1920, with the amount of historical research material available, was stark. We were shocked to learn about the ban in more detail: that it had essentially happened twice, and the involvement of the football authorities in misfeasance - at first encouraging and then putting a stop to the game.

Originally, we intended to find a local Edinburgh team to tell their story to a modern audience. However, it became clear that simply telling the tale of the ban and what had happened to the women's game before and since was what our play needed to be about.

All three of us are fathers to daughters. Learning about the struggle that women had to go through just to play a game of football and to be considered as equals in the sport was humbling for us. Our girls are now able to play and participate in football as a recognised choice, thanks to the struggle of those who have gone before them. There is today a pathway to professional status for women footballers, although the disparity with the men's game is still huge. There remains a long way to go.

We were mindful from the beginning that we were telling a story about women and so, very early in the process, we invited Heather Cochrane, Ria McLeod, Rachel Millar and Lucy Pedersen, all graduates of the acting course at Dundee & Angus College, to join us as a research team and to ensure the female voice was present throughout. Alongside Paul, Tim and I, they did a power of research into the period, the game and the teams. Furthermore, through workshopping and a number of readings they helped to give the characters their voice and all went on to become members of the original cast in the 2021 production. We are extremely grateful to them for their contribution.

Thanks are also extended to Nikki Auld, Hannah Howie, Lois Creasy and Gail Robertson for their input into the drafting process.

Once again, we were fortunate to be brilliantly supported in producing the show by Heart of Midlothian Football Club and all the staff at Tynecastle Park, especially given the challenges presented by the pandemic. Lianne Parry (Head of Heritage at Hearts) again went far above and beyond to help and support us – including answering emails on her holiday to make sure performances went ahead. We are so grateful to her for all her work to help us make the shows happen.

Finally, I'd like to extend my sincere thanks and appreciation to the original cast and behind the scenes team of *Sweet F.A.*: Natasha Murray, Eve Murray and Ian Cunningham, all of whom contributed enormously to the production and made it look and sound fantastic; the cast, with their love for the piece and support for each other, who made every day of rehearsal and performance a genuine joy.

Sweet F.A. was the very definition of brilliant teamwork and I am immensely proud to have worked with them all.

Come on the NBR!

Bruce Strachan

PROLOGUE

Gorgie, 1915. The Women enter.

Winning Working Women

All   [*Singing*] *We're aw women, working the war line*
We're aw women working overtime
We're aw women, playing till full time
We're aw women, mighty Scottish quines

We're aw women, working the war line
We're aw women working overtime
We're aw women, playing till full time
We're aw women, mighty Scottish quines

Winning working women won't you hear what
   we've tae say
We work our hands unto the bones, for a
   quarter less in pay
We started our own football teams and showed
   them how to play
But when we ask for equal rights we're given Sweet FA

All   [*Spoken*] Welcome to Tynecastle!

Helen Home of Heart of Midlothian Football Club!

Alice It's 1915.

Daisy Our boys in maroon finished the season second to Glasgow Celtic.

Harry Oh, they were gutted no tae win the league after winning 19 of the opening 21 games.

Mo But thirteen players volunteered tae fight in France.

Lil   They were the talk o' the toon...

Daisy   But that's a story for another time...

Helen   This is our story. The story of women's football.

Reenie   *Now, I ken what yer thinking.*

Lil   Women didnae play football!

Harry   They're busy having bairns, keeping hoose and knowing their place.

All   But play they did!

[*Singing*] *We're aw women, working like men folk*
We're aw women, we're aw in the same boat
We're aw women, 'Equal Rights' - (Ha ha) Good joke!
We're aw women, all we're asking for's the vote!

Winning working women, won't you hear what we've tae say
We've gained a shade of yellow skin, lost fingers, hair and taes,
But apparently we're 'far too frail' for that fitba' game to play
You take our graft, and take our limbs, and give us Sweet FA

Helen   [*Spoken*] It was the most popular game for a while. Until the Football Authorities stepped in.

The Women become the SFA: Lord Scunthorpe, Lord Dundee, Secretary Watt, Abercrombie, Buchanan and Campbell. They produce voting paddles that say 'AYE' on one side and 'NAY' on the other.

Lord Scunthorpe   All those in favour of stopping the women's game?

Each member raises his voting paddle to show 'AYE' and responds, apart from Lord Dundee.

All   Aye!

Lord Scunthorpe   Those against?

Lord Dundee *raises his paddle to show 'NAY'.*

Lord Scunthorpe   Are you sure? Perhaps you'd like to reconsider your vote, Lord Dundee?

They all turn and look at Lord Dundee, who sheepishly turns his paddle round.

Lord Scunthorpe   Resolution is hereby adopted. This, gentlemen, will put an end to this veritable curse!

All   Huzzah!

The Women become themselves once more.

Helen   Who'd have thought the footballing authorities could be corrupted like that?

All   [*Singing*] *We're aw women, football daft and crazy*
We're aw women, we'd play fae Perth to Paisley
We're aw women, united we will stand
We're aw women, but the blazers want us banned

Winning working women won't you hear what
    we've tae say
We work our hands unto the bones, for a
    quarter less in pay
We started our own football teams and showed
    them how to play
But when we ask for equal rights we're given...
We're given...
Sweet FA!

Alice   [*Spoken*] *So men* discouraged *women* playing.

Daisy   But times are changing.

Reenie With the men away fighting, we're picking up the
slack in the factories, making munitions and
supplies.

Mo   And works teams are forming all across the land.

Helen   We're bringing in the crowds and raising money for
the war effort.

Lil   And at the same time women are fighting their own
battle - a struggle for their rights - the right to vote,
the right to work.
The right to equality.

Reenie We'll get to all that the now, ladies and gentlemen.
But to kick off, our story begins with a chance
encounter in a well kent Gorgie establishment.
Scene One: The Athletic Arms!

All   Eh?

Reenie The Diggers!

All   Ah!

Reenie *exits.*

SCENE ONE

The Diggers

Daisy is standing at the bar. She is comfortable in her surroundings, although still wary. The rest don flat caps and become Men. Man 1 approaches Daisy.

Man 1   Hiya darlin'...can I interest you in my bone
collection?

Daisy   Nut!

Man 1 retreats as Alice enters. The Men jeer her as she comes in. Man 2 approaches her.

Man 2   Hiya darlin'...how would you like to see my bone
collection?...

Alice *is flustered.* **Daisy** *notices and steps in.*

Daisy   Bugger off!

Man 2 *retreats.*

Don't worry hen, some o' these clowns still think it's
the 1890s. You alright?

Alice   Yes. Thank you.

Daisy   Nae bother. Want a drink?

Alice   Oh, please allow me. My way of saying thank you.

Daisy   Won't say no to that...if we can get served that is!

Reenie, the factory supervisor, makes her entrance. She gains the attention of the bar.

Reenie Can I have your attention gentlemen! I ken I'm interrupting yer pints, lads...

Man 3 Hiya darlin'...can I interest you in my bone coll...

Reenie I'll break every bone in your body if you don't beat it right now! I work at the North British Rubber Company in Fountainbridge. We're now part of the war effort. And we need workers, since the laddies have gone tae France. We want yer women.

Man 3 Aye so do we...

Reenie Tell yer wives, sisters, daughters, grannies that we're recruiting.

Man 4 Whit's the wages like?

Reenie No as good as the men's, but good enough. The work is physically tough, but so are we.

Man 4 Tough as old boots!

Reenie Shut yer pus, you! Rest assured *we're* doing our bit tae help win the war. Can you men say the same? [*Pause*] Didnae think so. Spread the word. Any women wanting work can come down. Enjoy your afternoon...gentlemen.

Reenie eyes Daisy and Alice, standing at the bar. She goes to them.

Reenie Not often you see young women drinking in here.

Daisy [*Under her breath*] Not often you see auld women shouting in here.

Reenie What was that?

Daisy Nothing.

Alice This factory work…do you need a reference or something like that?

Reenie Only a good work ethic. [*To* **Daisy**] We can work on your attitude later. What's yer name?

Daisy Daisy.

Reenie [*Nodding at* **Alice**] And you?

Alice Alice.

Reenie Well, I encourage you to come along and get involved. We need to do our bit too. Monday, 9 o'clock sharp. Ask for Miss Brown.

Man 4 Hiya darlin'…

Reenie Get tae fu…

Man 4 Fair enough!

Reenie heads out, past the cowering Men.

Daisy First time in The Diggers then?

Alice Yes…Wait…The Diggers? The sign outside says The Athletic Arms.

Daisy Cemeteries on either side. Gravediggers drink here. Careful aboot chatting tae them.

Alice Ah…bone collection.

Daisy Aye, it's the only line they've got. Ever drunk beer?

Alice Of course! My family brew their own actually.

Daisy What's it called?

Alice McEwan's. Ever heard of it?

Daisy Err, I'd be drinking it, if I could get served!
So you must be rich!

Alice Hardly...

Daisy I bet you're fae Morningside or something.

Alice No. [*Pause*] Colinton. And you?

Daisy Fae Gorgie and proud of it.

Alice Thought so.

Daisy What's that mean?

Alice Your voice is...

Daisy Common?

Alice No! It's...real.

Daisy Real! That's a new one! Real!

Man 1 Right lads, nearly time for kick off, come on!

Men 'Mon the Hearts!

The Men leave the bar chanting.

Daisy So you winnae be interested in factory work? Being
posh an' aw that.

Alice I never said I was...

Daisy [*Smirking*] You dinnae need tae dirty yer hands wi the likes of us.

Alice Is that so?

Daisy [*Winding her up*] Toff's privilege. Pretending tae be working class, going to the boozer, telling daddy how fun it is tae be slumming it...

Alice My 'daddy' is a cripple. Polio. He can't work, and since my mother died, I've had to look after him. And he hates this, resents having his daughter mollycoddle him. Today when I presented him with lunch, he flung it across the kitchen. I had enough. Caught the first tram going anywhere, and as we passed this place I thought I needed a drink.

Daisy I'm sorry –

Alice And the brewery is my great uncle's, it's nothing to do with us...

Daisy We never did get that drink eh... I've got tae go.

Alice Where?

Daisy Tynecastle Park.

Alice You go to the games?

Daisy Aye. You like fitbaw?

Alice I used to kick a ball about with my brothers... but my father put a stop to it. Only boys play football. And I always thought: why?

Daisy Come to a game. Next best thing.

Alice I don't know...

Daisy   You'll love it. My husband Johnnie's always on at me tae let him ken how the team's daeing. He's away in France. As soon as the Hearts players volunteered, he went straight to the recruiting office and did the same. You got a sweetheart?

Alice   No, no.

Daisy   Well stick wi me – I'll find ye' a fellae! You coming?

Alice   Yes!

They begin to leave, as they do **Daisy** *stops and turns to the audience.*

Daisy   Scene Two. Away up in Gorgie!

SCENE TWO

Tynecastle Park

Alice and Daisy are watching the game. They are joined by the Men from The Diggers.

Yours Til You Die

All   Ohway, ohway, ohway, ohway!

Alice   [*Singing*]
I followed Gorgie Road
Past the trams and the mud
Past the boys selling papers
Past the bakers and the pubs

And just then it appears
As the mist departs
Tynecastle Park
Home of the Hearts

A promise of adventure
A thunder in the air
A gust of expectation
Fans appearing from a'wheres

Fathers with sons
Old lads together
Laughing and joking
No heed for the weather

My pace quickened
My heart racing
The crowds thickened
My mind elating

> *Yours till you die, yours till you die!'*
> *From the stadium comes the cry.*
> *'Yours till you die, yours till you die!'*
> *Now my heart knows the reason why.*
>
> *Through the turnstiles*
> *Onto the terraces*
> *Crammed with thousands*
> *Rapturous faces*

The music continues as an underscore, as Alice turns her attention to the game.

Alice   This is incredible! What a view!

Daisy   Well? What dae ye think?

Alice   I think I've just fallen in love.

Daisy   And it's yours till you die!

All   Come on the Hearts!

Daisy   What the hell is that, Hearts?! You're just sitting back watching them! Harry Graham – what's he playing at??

Man 1   Great ball! Well played.

Man 2   There he is! Get it oot wide!

Man 3   Make a run fer him, ya daftie!

Man 4   Get yer heid oan it!

Man 3   Wish we still had Paddy Crossan. He'd drive the team forward.

Daisy   Can't believe they're playing Graham again. He's bobbins.

Alice   [*Agreeing*] Bobbins.

Hearts score – the crowd roars.

Daisy   Yaaaass! Harry Graham! Always believed in you!

As the crowd celebrates, Alice and Daisy turn to the
audience and continue to sing:

All   [*Singing*]
      'Yours till you die, yours till you die!'
      From the stadium comes the cry!
      'Yours till you die, yours till you die!'
      Now my heart knows the reason why.

      The crowds are singing,
      My scarf is raised
      My ears are ringing
      Every voice in praise

      Can't move nor think
      Nor breathe nor hide
      I've never felt anything
      So raw and alive.

      'Yours till you die, yours till you die!'
      From the stadium comes the cry!
      'Yours till you die, yours till you die!'
      Now my heart knows the reason why.

The Men depart.

Alice   [*Speaking*] And we're all part of it, united as one
      body, one mind, one heart...the pace and the skill
      and the bravery and the passion and in the second
      half Willie Wilson scored another two goals and...
      They won and...and...I need this. I have to come
      back.

Daisy Some game eh!

Alice It was incredible!

Daisy I need tae go. Nice tae meet ye Alice!

Alice Wait! Will I see you next week?

Daisy We're away tae Partick Thistle next week!

Alice Well... Monday then?

Daisy What?

Alice At the factory. We could take those jobs?

Daisy ...

Alice Don't know about you, but I need the money.
And we'd be doing our bit for the war effort.
Working with a bunch of girls, it'll be a great laugh.
C'mon, I dare you!

Daisy Alright! Meet you Monday. 9 o'clock at the factory.

Alice See you then.

Daisy See you then.

Daisy *exits.*

Can't wait.

Alice exits. The rest of the Women enter.

SCENE THREE

The Factory

The Factory. Mo, Helen, Harry and Lil enter. Guitar underscores the scene.

Helen So the factories are getting new workers.

Harry All across Scotland a new female industrial workforce is appearing.

Reenie Helping the war effort.

Mo We didn't get as much pay as the men.

Harry Same bloody work though

Lil Aye...our fight was just beginning!

Helen In 1856, two savvy bootmakers...

Lil Henry Lee Norris.

Harry And Spencer Thomas Parmelee.

Helen Bought some land at Fountainbridge and built what became...

All The North British Rubber Company!

Mo Welcome to the factory!

Harry Scene three if yer counting!

Mo We make everything here.

Lil Hoses.

Mo Hot water bottles.

Lil And Wellington boots.

Mo That's our focus right now.

Helen You see, it rains a lot in France.

Harry All the bloody time apparently.

Lil So we are doing our bit.

Mo Keeping the boys' feet dry.

Harry But there are a lot of feet...

Lil So we need all the help we can get.

Helen So they can win the war.

Mo And our boys can come home.

During the last few lines, Reenie enters, holding a clipboard and pencil.

Reenie Well, they won't win the bloody war if you don't make the boots, will they? Back to work!

The Women exchange looks, none too happy at Reenie's outburst, but get back to work. As they do, Alice and Daisy enter.

You're late! [*Looking at her clipboard*] Alice McEwan? And Daisy Roberts? Your age, Miss McEwan?

Alice Twenty-two.

Reenie [*To Daisy*] And you?

Daisy   Twenty-seven. And it's Robertson.

Reenie shoots Daisy an icy glance. After a beat, she corrects the name in her clipboard.

Reenie Robertson. Twenty-seven. Right. I'm Miss Brown
          and I'm the supervisor here. If you are polite,
          punctual and hardworking, we won't have any
          problems. The girls will show you the ropes.

Alice and Daisy nod but remain where they are, unsure what to do.

          Well, on you go then!

Mo   Alright, Reenie, I'll look after them…

Reenie My name is Renée. And I'll thank you to call me
          Miss Brown in the workplace…Mrs Jardine.

Mo   [*Putting on a well-spoken voice with a hint of
          sarcasm*] Of course, Miss Brown. I shall see to it that
          the ladies are dressed in the appropriate attire and
          attend to their duties presently.

The ladies stare each other down for a moment. Harry and Lil resume their kickabout.

Reenie See that you do. I'm off to see the Manager.

Reenie [*Skilfully traps the ball and flicks it up into her
          hands*] And I'm taking this bloody ball away. You'll
          get it back at lunchtime.

Reenie exits as Harry and Lil give her evils.

Mo   [*To Alice and Daisy*] Dinnae worry aboot her. Her
          bark's worse than her bite. Welcome lassies! I'm
          Maureen. Pleased tae meet ye.

Alice/Daisy   Hello Maureen.

Mo   Call me Mo, everyone else does! This is Harriet Harper and Lily McKenzie.

Harry   Harry.

Lil   Lil.

Alice   So, you get to play football here?

Harry   Well, there's no a team.

Lil   But we have a kickaboot at lunchtimes.

Harry   Aye. Men versus women.

Lil   We see who can kick the ball through the wee cloakroom windaes.

Harry   If the men win, we buy them a pack o' Woodbines.

Lil   If we win, they buy us a bar o' Five Boys chocolate!

Daisy   Are ye any good?

Harry   Let's just say we'll no' be buying chocolate for the foreseeable future!

Mo   And that's Helen Matthews.

Helen   Hello girls.

Mo   And that's Ann and Rosie. They dinnae say much, but they sound great!

Daisy   Hiya! [*Gestures offstage*] What's the matter wi' Miss Broon?

Harry   Who, Reenie?

Helen   Dinnae let her hear you call her that.

Lil   Ken. [*Mocking*] It's *Renée*.

Mo   She's always like that. Don't think I've seen her crack a smile since I started here.

Lil   Naebody kens much aboot her.

Harry   Aye, keeps hersel' tae hersel'.

Lil   Probably goes hame to an empty hoose.

Mo   Eh...I go hame to an empty hoose!

Lil   That's no' what I meant. Her hoose was probably empty *before* the war started.

Helen   Alright girls. She's still yer elder.

Lil/Harry   Sorry Helen.

Alice   I like the name Renée, though. It's lovely.

Harry   It has a certain *je ne sais quois* right enough.

Lil   Whit does that mean?

Harry   [*Translating*] 'I don't know what.'

Lil   Why did you say it then?

Helen   Right girls, we'd better get tae work. We sole and line the boots. Very important.

Lil   Aye. We cannae hang *a-boot*.

Harry Terrible…Right! Let's gie it some *wellie*…

Lil That wisnae much better!

Harry Et tu, *boot*-ay!

Mo You could say we're the soul o' this company.

Harry Aye. Right doon the bottom covered in sh…

Helen Eh, that's enough! Come on, we'll show you. Mo?

Mo, **Harry** and **Lil** *go through the motions of work, demonstrating the process, as* **Helen** *helps* **Alice** *and* **Daisy**. *They sing a call and response waulking song, 'Cats and Dugs', which* **Alice** *and* **Daisy** *join in with after the first verse.*

Cats and Dugs

Mo *It's raining cats and dugs in France, (It's raining cats and dugs in France)*
The Kaiser doesnae hae a chance, (The Kaiser doesnae hae a chance)
For wi' the boys we're in cahoots, (For wi' the boys we're in cahoots)
Making aw the welly boots! (Making aw the welly boots)

Lil *Singing songs tae pass the time, (Singing songs tae pass the time)*
Working on the 'sembly line, (Working on the 'sembly line)
To win the war, oor common goal, (To win the war, oor common goal)
Tae help wi' all oor heart and soul! (Tae help wi' all oor heart and soul)

Harry *We're fightin' on a diff'rent front, (We're fightin' on a diff'rent front)*

> Tae help the boys gie Bill a shunt, (*Tae help the boys*
> *gie Bill a shunt*)
> *The shells explode, the rifles shoot, (The shells*
> *explode, the rifles shoot)*
> *The boys are steadfast in their boots! (The boys are*
> *steadfast in their boots)*

All *It's raining cats and dugs in France,*
The Kaiser doesnae hae a chance,
For wi' the boys we're in cahoots,
Making aw the welly boots! (It's raining cats and
dugs in France!)

*As the song ends, **Reenie** enters, studying her clipboard.*
She has the football under her arm.

Reenie Can I have your attention ladies?

Mo [*To the audience*] This is aboot three weeks later.

Reenie That includes you, Miss Harper. Right. It has been
decided by the factory management that due to a
rising- and quite frankly baffling- demand, a works
football team will be assembled. As well as players,
we need volunteers to run the team and organise
events, the aim of which will be to raise money for
the war effort. If you are interested you can sign up
here.

Reenie *holds out the clipboard.* **Harry** *rushes forward to take*
*it, but **Reenie** pulls it out of reach.*

> But... I must stress the importance of your work
> commitments. If you sign up for this ludicrous
> endeavour, you must not let it affect the production
> line. Do we understand each other?

Harry Can we have oor ball back, Mrs?

Reenie gives the football to Harry, and the clipboard to Lil, who scribbles her name on the sheet. Reenie exits. The Women continue to work and blether.

Harry   Oh ya beauty! A team! A real team!

Helen   Have you done this before?

Harry   I used to wander down to Gorgie for a kickaboot when I was wee. Used to skin the older lads, it was great fun.

Alice   Lucky you! My brothers would go off their heads when I tried to join in.

Harry   Are they away fighting?

Alice *nods.*

Harry   Well...they cannae go off their heads then! Fancy it?

Alice   I have to get home after work, I care for my father...

Lil   Well, if we can practise straight after work, you won't be home that late?

Alice   [*Thinks for a moment*] Yes! Why not!

Lil   Have you played before? In a real team, I mean.

Alice   Nope...how hard can it be though? Men play it all the time!

Harry   [*Holding the clipboard out*] Daisy?

Daisy reaches out to take the clipboard, then hesitates.

Alice   I thought you'd be desperate to sign up.

Daisy   It's just…I don't know what Johnnie would say…

Harry   Johnnie's no' here.

Lil   Aye. And even if he was, so what?

Alice   You'll be doing your bit for the war effort.

Daisy   [*Smiling*] Well, my country needs me, I suppose. I'm in!

Harry   Welcome to the team!

Helen   I'm no' playing, but I'll volunteer tae help oot.

Lil   D'ye ken much aboot football?

Helen   A wee bit. I played a little when I was younger.

Lil   Ye' never did!

Harry   Yer no' still playing are ye'?

Helen   Course I'm no'!

Alice   Who did you play for?

Helen   Mrs Graham's Eleven.

Daisy   Mrs Graham? Who was she?

Helen   She was me.

Harry   Eh?

Lil   But you're Helen *Matthews*.

Helen   'Mrs Graham' was a pseudonym.

Daisy   A what?

Alice   A made-up name.

Daisy   Why?

Helen   We thought it safer to protect our identities. But I
wish we'd been brave enough to proclaim publically
who we were.

Alice   Where have you played?

Helen   All over! The women's game was hugely popular...
we drew big crowds! In 1881 we played the very first
international, for Scotland against England, at
Easter Road...

Daisy   Boo!

Helen   We won. Three goals to nil. We had a rematch in
Glasgow the following week. But the crowd rioted.
Men went mad, tried to proposition us. Newspapers
accused us of incitement. We went on tour, playing
men's teams. There were more riots. I received a
black eye once.

Lil   Bloody hell! Were you alright?

Helen   Oh aye...I gave him two in return! But we had to
stop. The Scottish football authorities banned
women from playing.

Alice   What?

Helen   Well, it wasn't a ban as such...but we were
discouraged. Blatant discrimination against women.
I've missed it though!

Lil   Well this is your comeback! That just leaves Mo.
[*To Mo*] You game?

Mo   Eh...no. [*The rest protest*] Girls, I've no' kicked a
           ball in my life, I'm no' starting now.

Lil   Are you sure? It'd keep ye oot the empty hoose.

Alice Who do you have away fighting, Mo?

Mo   My husband, Jimmy. Two brothers. And my wee boy,
           David.

Alice Your *wee* boy?

Mo   Well, he's this height. [*She puts her arm above her
           head and stands on her tiptoes*] But he'll always be
           my wee boy.

Daisy [*To Helen, Harry and Lil*] What about you?

Harry My old man.

Lil   My fiancé, Jack.

Helen Nobody.

Mo   It might be nice to get oot the hoose right enough. I
           miss the noise. I cannae bear the quiet. Some folk
           would think it peaceful. No' me. I cannae sleep for
           listening to the silence.

Lil   I'm sorry Mo, I didnae mean tae upset ye...

Mo   It's alright hen. Life goes on eh. Tell ye what I
           dinnae miss though. The mess. He's clarty. No
           sooner is he oot the bath, he's covered wi' muck.
           I'm forever darning his clathes. He's always eating
           too. No sooner has he had his tea, he's wanting a
           piece. And I have tae drag him oot o' bed in the
           mornings, get him dressed, wash his neck...

Daisy   How old is he?

Mo   He's forty-six! My boy's no' much better either...Do you know what? To hell with it! Put my name doon!

Harry   That's the spirit Mo!

Mo   But like I said, I've never kicked a ball. And I cannae run that fast.

Lil   Nae bother...you can be the keeper! You dinnae have tae run then!

Mo   Suits me, hen! But I'm no' even sure what the rules are.

Harry   Ye have tae kick the ball in the opponent's goal.

Lil   Keep the ball and score one more than the other team.

Mo   I ken that!

Daisy   If your team has the ball, the other team cannae score.

Mo   When ye put it like that...

Alice   And Helen's played before, apparently she's going to coach us...

A whistle blows. Helen appears, the whistle round her neck. She is louder and stricter than before, like a different person.

Helen   [*As Mrs G*] Ladies! I am here to whip you into shape and get you playing football. As far as you are concerned, I am the gaffer around here.

All   Yes gaffer!

Helen   Let's begin!

Training Session One. Helen barks orders. The Women do their best, but are uncoordinated and clumsy. Afterwards, the Women are visibly tired and in some pain.

Helen   [*As Mrs G*] Well ladies. Could be worse, I suppose. But we really must work harder if we are to stand a chance. [*As Mrs M*] I'll see you tonight, Lil! Bye-bye girls!

Helen *exits.*

Lil   Is anyone else coming to the rally tonight?

Alice   We saw the last one on Gorgie Road, it was inspiring! Wasn't it Daisy?

Daisy   [*Distracted*] Hmm.

Lil   Well, it was until the authorities stepped in with their batons. It was meant to be a peaceful protest! Dinnae let that put ye off though.

Alice   Another time. I need to get home.

Mo   What's this?

Harry   Suffrage rally.

Mo   No thanks hen, I've suffered enough. [*To* **Lil**] Nae running you said! I'll sleep well the night... see you the morn. [*Quietly to Alice*] I'll bring some soup in for you and your dad tomorrow.

Alice   Oh, no, don't go to any trouble.

Mo   It's no trouble hen. Just keepin' a wee eye on ye.

Mo *exits. Alice pulls up her skirt and adjusts her stockings, which distracts Harry.*

Lil   Harry?

Harry   Eh...I can't tonight.

Alice   Shame. It's quite the experience.

Harry   Aye. Next time.

Alice   Goodnight.

Harry and Lil exit. Harry comes back in, as in her flustered state she has forgotten to take her pinny off.

Harry   Night Alice!

Harry exits. Alice and Daisy are alone. There's an unspoken tension between them.

Alice   I'll see you tomorrow, Daisy.

Daisy   I got a letter from Johnnie.

Alice   Is everything alright?

Daisy   They've been marched back from the front.

Alice   That's a good thing, isn't it?

Daisy   Aye. But his letter was strange. He sounded different. I just have a feeling something's wrong. I ken that sounds stupid...

Alice   No. No it doesn't.

Daisy   I think he hates being in France. Being a soldier.

Daisy is on the verge of tears. Alice hugs her.

Alice   Come on. Let's go for a cuppa tea. Shall we?

Daisy *nods. They exit, as Helen enters the space.*

Helen   And so it was I started coaching again. Oh, how I'd missed it! The women were eager, but they were far from a finished article. Conscription came to pass in March 1916, meaning more women were working and more football teams were born! I was to arrange some matches with neighbouring work places, but I felt my team should play a match behind closed doors first. A friendly lunchtime game of 7-a-side between themselves. It was successful. For the most part... [*She blows her whistle*] Scene Four! Boot Camp!

SCENE FOUR

Boot Camp

The Women enter, dishevelled and muddy. Daisy is fuming. Harry is limping.

Lil   That was great eh?

Mo   Aye, it was!

Harry   Who's that cow that booted me? Works in the canteen...looks like one o' they melted wellies in the reject bin.

Mo   What, Big Mary?

Harry   Aye! She just about broke my bloody leg!

Lil   You need tae toughen up, Harry!

Harry   She only did it cos I skinned her. I've seen milk turn quicker than her!

Mo   It's nice tae be oot the hoose. And meet some o' the other women properly. You dinnae always get the chance to speak to folk in other sections.

Daisy   Maybe you would've kept that last goal oot if ye werenae chattin' tae Agnes fae the typing pool.

Harry   Well, I'll be chattin' to Big Mary when I see her the morn, no mistake.

Mo   For Heaven's sake girls, it doesnae matter...

Harry   It does!

Mo   It's only a game!

Lil   Ken. Speaking o' which... [*Nodding to Daisy*]

Alice   You alright Daisy?

Daisy   I was never offside! That last goal would have won the game!

Alice   It was a training game.

Lil   Aye, it's only a kickaboot, it doesnae matter.

Daisy   It does!

Lil   I'd hate to see you if a decision doesnae go your way in a proper game!

Alice   And you *were* offside...

Daisy is raging. During the following exchange, Helen enters and watches from a distance.

Daisy   WHAT?

Alice   Well, you were.

Daisy   I wasnae!

Lil   Calm doon Daisy!

Harry   It was a close call, to be fair. But ye' were offside.

Daisy   I wasnae!

Harry   Ye' were!

Daisy   How would you know? You were too busy limping around the other end of the field...

Lil   Settle doon, it doesnae matter...

Daisy/Harry   It does!

Mo   What does *offside* mean?

Alice   [*To* **Daisy**] You need to drop it.

Daisy   I'm only sticking up for mysel'... Somebody has tae!
And if anyone's got a problem wi' that...

The Women start arguing loudly. Helen blows her whistle.
The Women fall silent.

> Ladies! This is NOT how a team conducts itself! You
> have to learn that the referee's decision is final. You
> must respect their decisions if you are to have integrity.

Daisy   [*Calmer now*] But what if the decision is wrong?

Helen   Welcome to Scottish football. [*As Mrs M*] Right, who
wants a brew?

The Women nod and Helen exits.

Mo   Jeezo, no wonder folk get worked up at the fitbaw!

Silence

Daisy   Sorry girls. I took that too far.

Lil   [*Laughing*] Did ye, aye?

Harry   It's fine hen. [*Putting her arm round Alice*] We
didnae take offence, did we?

Alice giggles at this. Daisy notes this, though the Women do
not. Helen enters with a teapot and mugs on a tray and a tin
full of chocolate bars. The Women get wired in.

Mo Ooh, lovely. Pass us one o' they chocolate bars would ye'?

Helen *throws a bar over to Mo, who drops it on the floor.*

Harry You'd better keep up the practice, hen!

Mo Aye, aye. Here, what is that offside thing anyway? Jimmy and David moan about it a lot. They tried tae explain it tae me once...

Helen A player is in an offside position if they are between the opposition goalkeeper and the last two defenders. [*To the audience*] And before anybody says anything, that *was* the actual offside rule in 1916. It was changed to one defender in 1925!

Daisy Aye. Then, if that player touches the ball, that player is deemed offside. [*To Alice*] Which I wasnae.

Alice And it's a free kick to the other team.

Mo Is that it? That's really easy tae understand. Jimmy and David tried tae explain it tae me at the dinner table. They were using salt and pepper shakers and sauce bottles, tae represent the players, ken. I didnae have a bloody clue what they were on aboot.

Lil Jack was the same! Except he used cutlery. Hearts were knives, Hibs were forks and the goalkeeper was a spoon.

Reenie enters, eyeing the Women suspiciously.

Daisy Whit?

Harry Why do they insist on using utensils? What arses!

Daisy Ken. And ye see how often the players get caught

offside in a game? The men dinnae seem tae understand it either!

Reenie Ladies, five minutes and you're back upstairs. You're on the clock. Mind what I said about that ridiculous game distracting you.

Reenie turns her attention to the ledger in her hand.

Mo Aye. I must say girls, I enjoyed that kickaboot. I'm starting to see what all the fuss is aboot. Jimmy and David always go to Tynecastle when Hearts are at home. They sometimes go to Easter Road too. In fact, they signed up for the war because o' the players volunteering.

Reenie stops in her tracks, distracted by what Mo is saying. The others do not notice her reaction.

They went up to the Usher Hall to see them wi' that George McCrae. They signed up that night.

Lil Aye, the Sporting Battalion! Jack was the same. Well, he prefers Hibs, being a Leither. He signed up at Castle Street wi' his pals.

Daisy Johnnie and his mates did the same.

Alice And my brothers.

Harry My old man too.

Lil Isn't it funny that the war brought them all together? Like us, I suppose. I know they probably dinnae ken each other, but it's nice to know they're all together.

Helen Aye. Looking after each other eh?

Lil   Aye. I cannae wait for Jack to come hame. Then we can get married. [*To Daisy*] How long you been wi' Johnnie?

Daisy   Two years.

Lil   Best two years o' yer life eh?

Daisy   [*Sarcastically*] Aye. Of course.

Harry   What about you and Jimmy, Mo?

Mo   Nearly twenty-five years now.

Harry   Love's young dream...Here, I can picture you greetin' on your wedding day!

Mo   I didnae. I've been greeting ever since though!

The Women laugh. Reenie suddenly bursts into tears. The Women stop, not knowing how to react.

Mo   Someone gie her a seat.

The Women are still frozen, staring at Reenie, as Mo goes to her.

            Well, on you go then! Harry. Tea. Come on Miss Brown, sit down.

Lil *grabs a stool and hurriedly brings it over.*

Reenie [*Sitting*] I'm fine.

Mo   Yer no'. Why don't you tell me what...

Reenie [*Interrupting*] I said I'm FINE!

Mo turns to go and stops herself. She pulls a white hanky from her sleeve, turns and holds it out. Reenie eventually softens and takes it.

Reenie   Thank you Maureen.

She accepts the tea from Harry. Harry holds up a chocolate bar as well, which Reenie shakes her head at.

>Robert...my boy...was at the Usher Hall that night. He's away with the Pals battalion and aw. He wanted tae go with the players. Hearts daft.

Mo   I had no idea.

Reenie   You weren't to know. I never said. My husband... my Andrew...volunteered. Before Robert did. The Cameron Highlanders were recruiting at Tynecastle after a match. He sent Robert home after the game and signed up there and then. Robert was furious when he found out. He wanted to volunteer too, but I said he was too young. He's only fifteen. Just a daft laddie.

>Then he went up to the Usher Hall a couple of weeks later. The recruitment officer sent him to the back of the queue and told him, 'You'll be nineteen when we ask you again, son'.

>My Andrew was proud of him. Told me not to worry, it'll all be over by Christmas, he said.

>And I had to stand by Andrew, because...well, he is my husband.

>Was...

>He was killed in the Battle of Loos. Last September. And my boy is in France now. On his own. Who knows where, he cannae write.

>Bloody men and their bloody football! If it wasn't for that stupid bloody game...

Mo They would have volunteered anyway.

Reenie I miss them. I miss the noise around the hoose.

Mo I ken what ye mean.

Reenie I'm sorry.

Mo Dinnae be daft.

Reenie I am. And I'm sorry for the way I've behaved. I see you all managing so well. Laughing and joking... I don't know... I was jealous. That you cope.

Mo We dinnae always. It's hard. I still find myself going into David's room to wake him up in the morning. It's hard when a habit gies ye pain. But it's fine tae feel like that. I'd be worried if ye didnae. And we have each other. Eh girls? And we're here for ye.

Reenie Thank you, girls. Thank you... Mo.

Mo You're welcome, Renée.

Reenie Call me Reenie. It's what my Andrew called me.

Mo Come on. I'll make ye some soup. It'll solve all yer worries.

Mo puts her arm around Reenie.

Reenie How's the football going?

Mo Nae idea hen, I dinnae ken what's going on. But I've made some pals.

Mo and Reenie exit. Ann enters. She gives a bag and a letter to Helen.

Helen Ladies. I have some good news. We have our first match arranged. We will be playing the Broxburn Oil Company on Sunday next. Away. Also, I have borrowed some strips befitting of the finest team in town.

The Women are delighted. Helen pulls a green football shirt from the bag. The Women's delight disappears.

Daisy Nut. I'm no' wearing that!

Helen Well, Miss Robertson, you'd better improve at the next training session - or you will be!

Training Session Two. The Women are more coordinated now. Half way through, Mo and Reenie enter and join in.

Helen [*As Mrs G*] Superb session tonight ladies. We shall overcome the Broxburn Oil Company on Sunday! Victory shall be ours!

All Yes gaffer!

Helen [*As Mrs M*] See ye's later on!

Helen *exits.*

Lil Bye Helen! Will we see you at the rally tonight girls?

Alice Yes! My father will cope for a little while longer.

Mo What a way to spend your birthday, Alice!

Alice The cause continues, birthday or not.

Mo I thought all they rallies had been stopped cos o' the war?

Lil Course no'! Just some of the more militant

activities. But our fight continues. [*Theatrically*] 'Let us show ourselves worthy of citizenship whether our claim to it be recognised or not!'

Harry You been rehearsing that?

Lil Well, Millicent Fawcett said it first.

Mo Bravo hen!

Reenie I'll be there too. No point rattling around in an empty house, eh Mo?

Mo Exactly Reenie!

Alice That's great Miss Br... Reenie.

Mo and Reenie exit. Harry has been hovering in the background. Lil approaches her.

Lil Ask her then.

Harry I'm gonnae.

Lil Go on then!

Harry I'm gonnae!

Harry walks to Alice, but her confidence evaporates. She swiftly doubles back to Lil.

I cannae!

Lil Right. I'll dae it for ye' then!

Lil approaches Alice.

Lil Alice... I'm bringing a... friend along tonight.

Alice   Wonderful!

Lil   Aye. She's a lovely lassie. Bit shy, mind.

Alice   Wait, what?

Lil   I think you'd *really* get along.

Alice   You think I'm…But I'm not…

Lil   Smashing! It's settled. See ye later!

Alice   But I'm not…

Lil smiles at Harry as she exits. Harry gives Alice an embarrassed wave before running out.

Daisy   It doesnae bother me if you are, y'know.

Daisy holds out a small parcel to Alice.

Alice   Is it that obvious?

Daisy *raises her eyebrows and smiles.*

Daisy   Anyway, happy birthday!

Alice   You didn't have to…

Daisy   I wanted to. Open it, then!

Alice opens the parcel to reveal a hand-knitted Hearts scarf.

Welcome tae the family!

Daisy takes the scarf and puts it round Alice's neck.

Alice   I love it! Thank you.

Daisy And I wanted to say thank you.

Alice For what?

Daisy [*Embarrassed*] For... bein' my pal.

Alice You're welcome.

They look at each other for a long moment.

Alice Shall we?

Daisy Aye. I'll do your hair for ye. Get you looking your best for Harry!

Alice Leave it, you! Come on.

Alice and Daisy exit. Helen enters from the opposite side.

Helen [*To the audience*] Meanwhile, miles away in a dark and foreboding room, a sinister clutch had gathered by candlelight, with murky deeds afoot. Ladies and gentlemen... I give you... the Baddies in Blazers... the Hoodlums from Hampden... Scottish Football's top brass... the Shady Footballing Authority! We'll call them the SFA for short.

Disclaimer: The Shady Footballing Authority is a work of fiction. Any similarities to persons connected with the Scottish Football Association and the Scottish Professional Football League are purely coincidental. Ladies and gentlemen... the SFA!

Helen winks at the audience as the Women enter as the SFA in a ritualistic procession. They carry their voting paddles, with the exception of Lord Dundee, who is empty-handed. Helen encourages the audience to boo. They sing 'The SFA Song', upbeat Copacabana style.

The SFA Song

All   *Want a last minute pen?*
Or a match rearranged?
It's no problem when
A small favour's exchanged!

We kick up our heels,
While we stifle appeals,
It's wheels within wheels
Within wheels within wheels!

Corruption is oozing,
While boozing and schmoozing,
Position abusing
Is jolly amusing,

The conduct's bemusing
And often confusing,
Down at the SFA!
To acknowledge your team,

You must come from the West,
And in blue or hooped green
You must always be dressed!
We paint the town red,

While the fans are misled,
The source of our bread's
In the papers we shred!
Corruption is oozing,

While boozing and schmoozing,
Position abusing
Is jolly amusing,
The conduct's bemusing
And often confusing,
Down at the SFA!

Lord Scunthorpe   Best of order! Best of order! Welcome my brethren! Welcome to Hampden. Do you have the agendas, Secretary Watt?

Secretary Watt   Yes, Sir. The meeting of the Shady Footballing Authority is now in session, the honourable Lord Neil Scunthorpe presiding.

Lord Scunthorpe   Excellent. Hand them out, would you?

Secretary Watt   It's my dutiful pleasure, Sir.

Lord Scunthorpe   Item One. Our new bespoke silken blazers will be arriving soon, winging their way from the finest sweatshop this side of Persia. We shall look quite the thing down at the club, eh?

Secretary Watt   Especially you, Sir.

Lord Scunthorpe   Item Two. How is our 'Progress the West' initiative coming along?

Campbell   The initiative is fine; we're giving each of the Old Firm their own end of the national stadium; Celtic the East end and Rangers the West...

Lord Scunthorpe   Well, those are the cup finals we all want to happen!

Buchanan   We're ensuring all our referees are from the West of Scotland...

Abercrombie   Which will ensure that reprimands, cards, etcetera should be kept to a minimum.

Campbell   In fact, while we're at it, I suggest that Old Firm captains are given carte blanche within standard rules and regulations.

Lord Scunthorpe Yes, quite!

Buchanan It's not enough! Let the record show that at least one penalty per game is to be awarded to the Old Firm by the season's completion.

All Hear hear!

Lord Scunthorpe Yes...That horrible team from Edinburgh came a little too close for my liking last year!

Abercrombie It's the name I have a problem with. 'Progress the West' implies we care about teams outside of Glasgow...Kilmarnock, Motherwell, St. Mirren...

Buchanan God forbid! If I had my way, the Old Firm would play each other thirty-eight times a season!

All At least.

Lord Dundee Well, how about we limit the initiative to teams from Glasgow?

All Are you mad?

Abercrombie What about Third Lanark?

Buchanan Queens Park?

Abercrombie & Buchanan Partick bloody Thistle?

All You really are a fool, Dundee!

Campbell How about...The 'Affirm the Old Firm' Initiative?

Lord Scunthorpe Brilliant! No confusion then! Secretary Watt, make the arrangements will you? And keep it under your hats, chaps?

Secretary Watt Of course, Sir, you can trust me. You can't spell 'Secretary' without 'Secret'!

They all guffaw, except Lord Dundee, who looks confused.

Lord Scunthorpe Item Three. Our associates at the English FA have an allegation of corruption and match fixing being brought against them, pertaining to the 1914-15 season. Would it be wise, therefore, to conduct an investigation...

All Are you MAD!?

Lord Scunthorpe An *internal* investigation of our own to pre-emptively prove we are honest and above board?

All Oh!

Lord Scunthorpe Goody! Who shall conduct the investigation?

Campbell I'll do it! [*Under his breath*] That means I can't be investigated.

Campbell *walks up the line, inspecting the others, who look terrified.*

Done. No corruption here!

All Huzzah!

Lord Scunthorpe Excellent! If there is no other business, we shall retire to the club.

Secretary Watt I'm terribly sorry, Sir, but there is one more thing...

All Bloody hell!

Lord Scunthorpe What is it, Watt?

Secretary Watt Item 4 Sir?

Lord Scunthorpe Gentlemen. A dark, dark shadow blights our beloved game...

Lord Dundee Sectarianism?

Lord Scunthorpe Don't be ridiculous, Dundee! It's wo... wo...wo...

Campbell Spit it out, Sir!

Secretary Watt Women's football.

Buchanan Women?!

Campbell Football?!

All   Outrageous!

Lord Dundee I don't understand...

Secretary Watt It has come to my attention that women's teams are cropping up in factories up and down the country!

Buchanan Teams?!

Campbell Factories?!

Abercrombie Outrageous!

Lord Dundee I don't understand...

Lord Scunthorpe I thought we'd put a stop to all that nonsense? Can't we just ban them again?

All   Ban them!

Secretary Watt   It's not that simple. We didn't technically ban them before, we just encouraged our members to refuse them the use of facilities. But there has been a resurgence and they *are* raising money for the war effort. People are really taking to the whole thing.

Lord Scunthorpe   Bloody wo...wo...wo...

Secretary Watt   Women...

Lord Scunthorpe   ...ruining my evening!

Secretary Watt   If I may? Perhaps we should let them keep playing...

All   Are you mad? You really are a fool, Watt!

Secretary Watt   But the addition of women to the workforce is having a positive effect on morale. Productivity in your factory is up. You would be seen as patriotic heroes.

Lord Scunthorpe   Wait a minute...What if we offered them our support?

All   [*Except Watt*] Ooh!

Abercrombie   Ooh...I like the sound of that!

Secretary Watt   Excellent idea, Sir.

Lord Scunthorpe   Motion is proposed! All those in favour of supporting this?

Each member raises his voting paddle to show 'AYE' and responds, apart from Lord Dundee.

All   Aye!

Lord Scunthorpe   Those against?

Lord Dundee *raises a hand.*

Lord Dundee   Um, sorry chaps…I seem to have lost my vote.

Lord Scunthorpe   Did you ask for another one, Dundee?

Lord Dundee   Yes! I did! But the bloody thing must have
          got lost in the post…

Lord Scunthorpe   No problem, Lord Dundee, you can have
          mine.

*Lord Scunthorpe hands Lord Dundee his paddle, who holds up
the 'NAY' side.*

Lord Dundee   Ban them!

Lord Scunthorpe   No, Lord Dundee, that's not what we
          want…must we do this every time?

*Lord Scunthorpe turns the paddle in Lord Dundee's hand to
show 'AYE'.*

Lord Scunthorpe   That's the stuff! Watt, find a match.
          We shall attend, give it the personal touch! We will be
          the champions of equality! Now…to the Gentlemen's
          Club!

All   Huzzah!

The SFA file out as Helen enters the space again.

SCENE FIVE

The Big Game

Helen   Scene five! The big game! We arrived in sunny Broxburn to a big crowd, more than the team were expecting. There was a hush on the journey. Mo didn't make a peep. Harry didn't crack a joke. You could tell there were nerves, though nobody would admit it. They looked quite the part in their strips. Like a proper team.

The Women enter in their maroon strips.

Daisy   Much better colour, gaffer!

Helen   The women discussed important tactical matters while getting ready.

Daisy   Here, should we be using some of those...och... what's the word?

Alice   What word?

Daisy   For a made up name? [*To Helen*] Mind, you used them when you played before...

Helen   A pseudonym?

Daisy   Aye!

Mo   What you on aboot?

Daisy   Will we need to make up names?

Harry   Why would we dae that?

Alice   Women had to do it before, to protect themselves.

Reenie Folk won't be bothered will they?

Helen No, we'll be alright.

Harry Aye, most folk will be thankful we're helping the soldiers.

Mo That's a shame. I quite fancy having a new name, it would be exciting.

Lil What would you all choose?

Reenie I think I would choose something like Joan Smith.

All Joan Smith?

Reenie I just want an ordinary name for a change.

Lil I think I'd be Theda Bara.

Harry Theda Bara?

Daisy The film star?

Lil Aye.

Reenie You cannae be Theda Bara.

Lil How no?

Daisy You just cannae!

Mo Aye. Folk might think she's playing.

Harry Aye. It's a well-known fact that when she's no' making films in Hollywood, Theda Bara enjoys a kickaboot in the Meadows.

Mo   On second thoughts, can I just be Mo Jardine? I like being mysel'.

Helen blows her whistle and the team gather round her.

Helen [*As Mrs G*] Ladies! You are on the verge of greatness. We are raising money for the war effort, and we must not lose sight of that. But today is historic for you. You will be the first group to represent the North British Rubber Company in its footballing endeavours. Follow the plan, get out there and get stuck in!

All   Come on the NBR!

The Women cheer and step forward. The following is said directly to the audience.

Daisy There's an almighty cheer from the crowd as we take to the field.

Alice We're kicking off.

Reenie Lil and Alice are over the ball.

Helen blows her whistle.

Helen We're off!

Lil   Straight from kick off, we're all over them.

Reenie Daisy gets the ball on the right wing.

Daisy Knocks it inside to Harry.

Alice Harry skins the left back and leaves him stranded.

Harry They're slower than a week in the jail.

Lil   She gets tae the byline and whips in a cross.

Mo   Lil just misses the connecting header.

Reenie But the ball bounces to Alice, who's sprinting in at the back post.

Daisy She puts her laces through it.

All   Goal!

Lil   Less than thirty seconds gone!

Harry They've no' even touched the ball yet!

Alice The gaffer isn't celebrating though.

Helen Concentrate! Keep the concentration!

Harry Sorry gaffer!

Lil   Sorry gaffer!

Alice So we do.

Lil   They restart and the game calms doon.

Mo   They start tae knock it about a bit, but we are pressing them.

Helen We're fitter than they are.

Reenie Harry puts their centre mid under pressure.

Harry And the cow boots me right in the shin!

Daisy Harry is in some pain, but straight back on her feet.

Lil   No complaints.

Reenie No fuss.

Harry No free kick! Ref!

Helen Now they're on the attack.

Daisy Their outside left cuts inside.

Alice Lining up a shot.

Mo Oot o' nowhere, in slides Big Mary!

Daisy She gets the ball but she clatters the winger in the process.

Harry God bless ye, Big Mary!

Alice Reenie picks up the ball on the edge of her own box.

Lil She knocks it on to Alice.

Mo Lays it off to Harry, who hits a shot.

Reenie Deflects off a defender.

Alice Loops over the keeper.

All Two nil!

Harry Ya beauty!

Helen blows her whistle.

Lil The full time whistle sounds.

Harry We are victorious!

Mo I didnae have a save to make!

Helen [*As Mrs G*] Ladies! Congratulations on raising a
substantial amount of money for the war effort!
And congratulations on a hard fought victory.

Lil Ach it wasnae hard fought!

Harry Ken! I've fought harder wi' sleep!

Helen Complacency is unbecoming. Your next match will
be an altogether greater challenge.

Daisy Who have we got next?

Helen You will be playing Ramage & Ferguson's Ladies.

Alice Ramage & Ferguson?

Mo The shipbuilders?

All Fae Leith?

Harry An Edinburgh derby?

Lil Bloody hell!

Helen Indeed. [*As Mrs M*] Exciting i'nt it?

Winning Working Women (Reprise)

All   [*Singing*]
We're aw women, football daft and crazy
We're aw women, we'd play fae Perth to Paisley
We're aw women, united we will stand
We're aw women, but the blazers want us banned

Helen   [*Spoken*] One game played, one game won. We were
off to a great start. But our next outing would be an
altogether different experience in more ways than one.
Brace yourselves for derby day...after the interval!

All   [*Singing*]
Winning working women won't you hear what
  we've tae say
We work our hands unto the bones, for a quarter
  less in pay
We started our own football teams and showed them
  how to play
But when we ask for equal rights we're given Sweet FA

Helen blows her whistle to signify halftime.

SCENE SIX

Leith Links

Helen enters and blows her whistle.

Helen I hope you've left something in the bar for us!
Time for the second half!

The Women enter, getting ready for the game. They sing, psyching themselves up.

Lace Up Our Boots

All *We toil on the work line to help fight the Hun,*
While the boys on the front line are having their fun,
We take to the football fields, playing our game,
They march into battle, but soon they'll come hame.
We're doin' our bit, tae help win the war,
Picked up the slack and discovered much more,
We pull on our strips now, as eager recruits,
It's time for us women to lace up our boots!
We welcome our rivals, with arms open wide,
Then send them packing, by tanning their hide,
We work hard and play hard, remember our name,
Don't try to tell us it's only a game!
We're doin' our bit, tae help win the war,
Picked up the slack and discovered much more,
We pull on our strips now, as eager recruits
It's time for us women to lace up our boots.
Come on the NBR!

The Women become the SFA, attending the derby match.

Helen A couple of weeks later, it was time for the derby.
We had some unexpected visitors.

Lord Scunthorpe What larks! Where are we, Watt?

Secretary Watt Scene six. Leith Links, Sir.

Lord Scunthorpe Never heard of it.

Lord Dundee Which part of Glasgow is that?

Campbell We're in Edinburgh, chaps.

They all show their disgust.

Secretary Watt Ramage & Ferguson's Ladies play North
      British Rubber Ladies.

All   I say!

Secretary Watt Equality, chaps!

Lord Scunthorpe Which one's what?

Secretary Watt I am Secretary Watt, Sir...

Lord Scunthorpe Don't be ridiculous, Watt! I mean which
      team is which!

Secretary Watt Ramage & Ferguson are greens,
      North British Rubber, the NBR, are maroons.

Buchanan Dreadful colours, not enough Royal Blue.

Abercrombie And the greens have no hoops.

All [*Except Watt*]   Ridiculous!

Lord Dundee Ban them!

Lord Scunthorpe No Dundee, we've been over this!

Helen blows her whistle near Campbell, who is deafened by the sudden noise.

Lord Scunthorpe Kick off!

Campbell What?

Secretary Watt Yes Sir?

Campbell What?

Secretary Watt I'm here, Sir!

Abercrombie Pipe down, Watt, we're trying to watch!

Buchanan The greens' outside left is tricky.

Abercrombie For a woman!

Campbell She left that big one standing!

Buchanan There's the cross.

Lord Scunthorpe The keeper has punched it away!

Campbell Perhaps she's scared of the ball!

Lord Scunthorpe Maroons are hitting it long.

Secretary Watt It's over the entire midfield.

Abercrombie And the defence!

Buchanan The little one's running on to the ball.

Campbell It's one on one.

Secretary Watt She scores!

Helen   One nil!

Secretary Watt   Wait…it's been disallowed!

Helen   Offside?

Campbell   Offside?

Abercrombie   What does that mean?

Secretary Watt   Free-kick to greens.

Lord Scunthorpe   The little one is shouting at the referee! What's she saying?

Buchanan   The referee's in banking?

All   Oh!

Helen   Daisy Robertson! Control yourself!

Secretary Watt   The greens are attacking.

Lord Scunthorpe   Another cross.

Secretary Watt   Everybody missed it.

Lord Dundee   Including the 'keeper!

Secretary Watt   The ball's trickled over the line.

Buchanan   What's happening?

Secretary Watt   Goal! One-nil greens.

Lord Dundee   The maroon 'keeper couldn't catch a cold!

Helen   Come on ladies! Keep the ball! Calm things down.

Abercrombie Yes, come on, girlies!

Buchanan Keep going, young fillies.

Lord Scunthorpe The maroons are on the ropes… Getting kicked off the park aren't they?

Helen blows her whistle.

Lord Scunthorpe Thank God that's over!

Secretary Watt It's only half time, Sir!

All What Watt?

Abercrombie I still can't fathom this bloody offside malarky…

Buchanan Right… [*Reordering where A and C are standing*] let's say you're the 'keeper, you're the forward and I'm the ball…

Lord Dundee Who can I be?

Buchanan You can be the defender!

Lord Dundee What does he do?

Buchanan He defends…

Lord Dundee I don't understand…

Abercrombie Oh, let's just go to the club chaps… to Glasgow!

All [*Except Watt*] Huzzah!

Lord Dundee, Abercrombie, Buchanan and Campbell exit.

Secretary Watt [*To Lord Scunthorpe*] We should stay, Sir. Talk to some of these women.

Lord Scunthorpe [*Childish*] But I want to go to the club!

Secretary Watt Patriotic heroes, Sir...

Lord Scunthorpe Oh, if we must! But I'll need a stiff brandy first.

Lord Scunthorpe and Secretary Watt leave. Helen blows her whistle.

Helen The second half was hugely frustrating. Neither team could score. The game ended one nil to Ramage & Ferguson's. Derby defeat. The girls are devastated. But that's football. We will dust ourselves down and go again. No excuses.

Helen exits as Alice and Harry enter.

Harry Well, I don't know about you, but I could drown my sorrows. Fancy coming to the Diggers with me?

Alice After that game? Absolutely!

Daisy enters.

Harry Right! It's a date then...

Daisy feels a pang of jealousy. Alice sees Daisy and becomes flustered.

Alice Daisy, do you want to come to the Diggers with us?

Harry realises she's barking up the wrong tree.

Harry Actually, I've just remembered I've forgot... something. You two have a nice night eh?

Harry *exits.*

Daisy   I don't feel up to it.

Alice   What's wrong?

Daisy   We lost. A derby. And I didn't play well.

Alice   For what it's worth, I didn't think you were offside…

Daisy   Johnnie's coming hame. He's been invalided oot ay France.

Alice   Oh…

Daisy   Him coming back changes everything…I like the way my life is.

Alice   I like the way your life is too.

Alice suddenly leans in to kiss Daisy, who backs off.

Daisy   Alice…

Alice   I thought you meant…

Daisy   I have a husband.

Alice   But you and Johnnie –

Daisy   I'm not…I can't.

Alice   I'm sorry.

Daisy   Alice…

Alice   What was I thinking? I feel so stupid.

Alice exits. Before Daisy can follow, Lord Scunthorpe and Secretary Watt enter.

Secretary Watt   Congratulations! A gallant player from the match, if I'm not mistaken?

Daisy   Err, aye.

Lord Scunthorpe   Jolly well done. Splendid footballage!

Daisy   What?

Secretary Watt   We're looking for your manager?

Daisy gestures to Helen, before going after Alice.

Lord Scunthorpe   Ah Madam! Do *you* know where the manager is?

Helen   I am the manager!

Lord Scunthorpe   But you're a wo...a wo...a wo...

Secretary Watt   [*Interrupting*] A wonderful example of the wonder of the women's game! This is Lord Scunthorpe, Chairman of the Football Authority, and I am Secretary Watt.

Lord Scunthorpe   We were told about your team, the Northern...Company for Rubbing...

Helen   North British Rubber Company.

Lord Scunthorpe   That's the fella! Capital display today. A quite splendid achievement!

Helen   We lost.

Secretary Watt Uh…Lord Scunthorpe means…forming a
football team.

Lord Scunthorpe Yes, especially given the fact that you're
all wo…wo…

Secretary Watt [*Interrupting*] Working in the factory at
the same time!

Lord Scunthorpe Heartening to hear the beautiful game is
thriving even among the wo…

Secretary Watt [*Interrupting*] War effort you are all
involved in! Football brings everybody together.

Lord Scunthorpe No matter which side of Glasgow you're
from…

Secretary Watt Sir…

Lord Scunthorpe Although the Old Firm rivalry is rather
thrilling…Hooray for 'whataboutery' and all that…
[*Patting his breast pocket*] keeps the money rolling in!

Secretary Watt Sir…

Lord Scunthorpe Where was I? Oh yes…Football unites us,
no matter the differences in class, background,
creed –

Helen And gender.

Secretary Watt We commend the growth of women's
teams!

Lord Scunthorpe Jolly good thing for morale. In France
our men fight valiantly, here at home their wo…
wo…wives do their bit. Brothers-in-arms and all
that.

Helen Sisters-in-arms.

Secretary Watt Precisely.

Helen But you stopped women playing the game.

Secretary Watt Regrettably, yes, but that was a long time ago...

Lord Scunthorpe And it was a complete farce.

Secretary Watt Sir...

Lord Scunthorpe Dangerous for the old reproductive whatnots...but I wouldn't expect a wo...lady person to understand...

Helen I beg your pardon?

Secretary Watt Keen on a rematch?

Lord Scunthorpe Different thing altogether.

Secretary Watt Against the Leith team?

Lord Scunthorpe You're not really...

Helen A rematch?

Secretary Watt You deserve a more fitting venue...

Lord Scunthorpe I mean, you're doing men's work...

Secretary Watt Somewhere like Tynecastle Park, perhaps?

Helen Well now...

Secretary Watt Let's see if something can't be arranged.

Lord Scunthorpe Even dressed like chaps...

Helen My team would love to play at Tynecastle.

Secretary Watt Say... Saturday next? First of July?

Lord Scunthorpe The social unrest it was causing.

Helen Show people what we can do. Perhaps change a few stubborn minds?

Lord Scunthorpe It was footballing Armageddon!

Secretary Watt Leave it with us.

Helen Actually... Would it be possible to get a sponsor involved in the rematch? It could help fill the charity coffers? Raise the profile a bit?

Lord Scunthorpe My dear wo... missy! The SFA does not have time for sp... sp...

Secretary Watt Sponsors?

Lord Scunthorpe [*Pointing at Secretary Watt*] That!

Secretary Watt Terribly nice to meet you, now we really must be going.

Lord Scunthorpe Now can we go to the club?

Secretary Watt [*To Lord Scunthorpe*] Yes! If you behave! [*To Helen*] Saturday next, first of July!

Secretary Watt escorts Lord Scunthorpe from the vicinity. A reprise of 'Lace Up Our Boots' strikes up.

SCENE SEVEN

Derby Delight

Lace Up Our Boots (Reprise)

All [*Singing*]
We welcome our rivals to Tynecastle Park,
The girls in maroon will be making our mark!
We'll put on a show, the best you've ever seen,
We're oot for revenge on the ladies in green!

Helen [*Spoken*] Scene seven. Derby delight!

All [*Singing*]
We're doin' our bit, we've got the belief,
We're gonnay batter the wee team fae Leith!
We pull on our strips now, nae messing aboot,
It's time for us women to lace up our boots!

Daisy [*Spoken*] Tynecastle Park.

Alice Saturday first of July 1916.

Reenie The day o' the big match.

Lil We got to use the dressing rooms and everything!

Harry We ran out of the tunnel.

Mo There must have been at least a thousand folk!

Reenie Mair like fifteen hundred.

Alice The press was there too.

Harry We had to pose for a photograph.

Lil I felt like Theda Bara!

The Women stand in a team photo pose. Alice and Daisy are next to each other.

Daisy [*To Alice*] How are you? Alice, talk to me.

Alice [*To Daisy*] I'm fine Daisy. Focus on the game.

Reenie There's a proper ref!

Mo And linesmen!

Helen *blows her whistle.*

All Come on the NBR!

Harry The Leithers are straight on the attack.

Mo Except this time, we are ready for them.

Alice The tricky outside left got the ball.

Reenie But Harry is dropping back to pressure her.

Harry And Big Mary's on her too.

Daisy It goes back to their 'keeper.

Mo And the ball gets booted up the park.

All Hoooof!

Harry Straight into Mo's arms!

Lil The ball is rolled out to Reenie.

Mo If we've got the ball, they cannae score!

Daisy It's knocked out to Alice on the left wing.

Reenie She knocks it past the full-back and runs on.

Mo Sees Daisy about to make a run into the box.

Lil Alice splits the defence with a swerving ball.

Harry The centre-backs are looking for offside.

Alice But she isn't! Daisy's played a blinder.

Harry She chips the ball over the incoming keeper.

All One nil!

Helen Don't focus on the crowd, watch the game, heads up!

Harry Sorry gaffer!

Lil Sorry gaffer!

Reenie Daisy is having a rare time on the right.

Harry The full-back cannae get close to her!

Lil She knocks the ball towards the near post.

Daisy Alice is running in, but she's too far out.

Harry Until she dives towards the ball.

Helen It's like she's floating on air!

Mo She nods it with her head.

Lil Goal!

All [*Except Alice*] Two nil!

Harry   Bravely done, Alice!

Mo   But she doesnae get up.

Lil   She's holding her shoulder.

Harry   Did she fall into the post?

Daisy   Alice?

Daisy helps Alice to her feet.

Alice   I'm alright, I can carry on! [*To Daisy*] Thank you.

Alice continues to play despite being in pain, clutching her shoulder.

Harry   Five minutes to go.

Daisy   They're on the attack.

Mo   That outside left's on it again.

Lil   She unleashes a shot fae the edge o' the box.

Reenie   But Mo dives doon to the far post and pushes it wide.

All   What a save!

Reenie   The corner comes in and Mo collects the ball.

Harry   Practice makes perfect hen!

Lil   She kicks it out.

Mo   Harry jumps and flicks it on with her head.

Harry   It falls to Daisy, who goes to turn one way, then spins the other.

Lil   She's lining up a shot.

Alice   She's too far out.

All   Dinnae hit it from there!

Alice   But she does!

All but Alice and Daisy freeze, as if time is standing still for them.

Daisy   The ball loops up.

Alice   It's moving in the air.

Daisy   And I'm…

Alice   And she's…

Daisy   The keeper's off her line.

Alice   Come on…

Daisy   Come on!

Alice   It hits the underside o' the crossbar.

Daisy   Hits the line.

Alice   And spins back into the net!

They embrace as the rest of the Women come back to life.

All   Yaaaaaas! Three nil!

Lil   What a finish!

Harry   I telt you to hit it fae there!

Helen blows her whistle.

Mo   Full time!

Lil   There'll be nae sunshine doon Leith way the day!

Helen   The second Edinburgh derby is ours! It's a triumphant day all round. There was a big push in France today, in the Somme region. By all accounts, our boys have done well.

Daisy   Things couldn't get much better.

Mo   Or so we thought.

Lil   The real truth about the big push and the Somme started to filter back home.

Harry   The newspapers drip fed the information to make it sound less horrific.

Reenie   It was less than a year since I'd lost my Andrew. I prayed for my boy. For all of us.

Helen   Over 60,000 British casualties.

Daisy   Over 20,000 men died on that 'triumphant' day alone.

Lil   Five times what the new Archibald Leitch stand can hold.

Mo   And back here, everywhere you turned, there was loss.

Harry   I lost my father.

Harry leaves the space.

Lil   I lost my fiancé.

Lil leaves the space.

Mo   I lost my husband and both my brothers.

Helen   But her son survived.

Mo   My wee boy!

Mo leaves the space.

Alice   I was lucky. Both my brothers were fine.

Reenie I lost my boy. Missing, presumed dead. I lost
        everyone.

Helen puts her arm round Reenie and they leave the space.

Daisy   And my Johnnie was hame.

Alice   In body, no' in mind.

Daisy   We continued to work.

Alice   For some of us, it was all we had left.

Daisy   Work.

Alice   Football.

Daisy   Each other.

Alice   Daisy and I were lucky enough to be selected as
        part of a Scottish XI and got to play against the
        famous Dick, Kerr's Ladies, here at Tynecastle.

Daisy   They were some team. Best in the country!

Alice Lily Parr was playing.

Daisy The most prominent and famous female footballer.

Alice The legendary Bobby Walker described her as:

Daisy 'The best natural timer of a football' he'd ever seen.

Alice She scored four goals.

Daisy We lost, but we raised £800 for military charities.

Alice And some of us made quite the impression…

Alice *leaves the space as* **Alfred Frankland** *enters.*

Frankland Miss Robertson?

Daisy Aye?

Frankland I'm Alfred Frankland, I run Dick, Kerr's Ladies.

Daisy It's a pleasure, Sir.

Frankland Your team played well today. We don't usually get run so close.

Daisy Aye, well we can maybe get a rematch organised, get oor revenge!

Frankland Indeed! I must say, yourself and the other winger, Miss McEwan, caught my eye.

Daisy Oh aye?

Frankland Aye! I have room in my squad for players of your quality. How would you like to play for me?

Daisy For Dick, Kerr's?

Frankland I can offer you a place in our team, a chance to play at a higher level, with women from all over. And of course, a job at our factory in Preston, lodgings...

Daisy Preston? I cannae...

Frankland Think it over at least?

Daisy The people I love are here and I can't leave them.

Frankland Bring 'em with you!

Daisy I cannae. I'm sorry, the answer's no.

Frankland Well family comes first. He's a lucky man.

Alice enters.

It's a shame you won't be partnering up with Miss McEwan in Preston. Best of luck, Miss Robertson.

Alfred Frankland shakes hands with Alice before leaving.

Daisy You're going?

Alice Of course!

Daisy What about...your father?

Alice I've been caring for him on my own for four years. It's my brothers' turn.

Daisy They won't let you leave.

Alice I'd like to see them try and stop me!

Daisy I didnae think you'd go.

Alice   What's wrong?

Daisy   I'm not going!

Beat

Alice   But this is a great opportunity...

Daisy   I can't.

Alice   You mean you won't.

Daisy   We don't all have it easy like you, Alice!

Alice   You think I have it easy? Why are you being like this?

Daisy   I'm no' being like anything.

Alice   Well, I'm not staying. The only thing that was
keeping me here was you.

*They are close together now. They stare at each other for a
moment.*

Daisy   Well, I'm not leaving. I'm married.

Alice   I thought...I thought you felt...

Daisy   Ye thought wrong.

Alice   Fine. Good luck, Daisy.

Daisy   [*Sarcastically*] Aye! Congratulations!

*A version of 'Yours Till You Die' plays. Alice and Daisy leave
the space as the rest of the Women enter.*

SCENE EIGHT

The Letter from Preston

The factory. Ann brings in two letters and a parcel for Reenie.

Helen [*To the audience*] Several months later. With Alice gone, we were a woman down. But the rest of us carried on, working and playing. There was no rest for some. Scene Eight. The Letter from Preston.

Harry We all training tonight, aye?

Lil I have to leave early, I've got a union meeting.

Mo Are ye' still involved in aw that suffrage stuff hen?

Lil Aye. There's reps from the Labour Party going tonight, they're behind us now.

Reenie I dinnae ken where ye' get yer energy from, hen!

Lil Cos it's important. It's more vital now than ever.

Mo You work too hard hen! A young lassie like you could be daein' somethin' mair fun wi' her spare time.

Lil D'ye hear yersel? I dinnae ken any women who can vote. Dae you?

Mo Well, no.

Reenie It's a start, hen.

Lil And I'm no stoppin' until every woman in every community has the right, including us!

Mo   Well, good for you!

Daisy   How's it men over the age o' twenty-one can vote
            and it's thirty for women?

Mo   And we have tae own property.

Harry   Dinnae forget men under twenty-one who fought in
            the war can tae.

Daisy   I ken the men did the fighting, but they'd no' have
            won withoot us women. Who made their wellies and
            their bullets?!

Lil   Aye. We did our bit. Our fight is just beginning!

Reenie gives one of the letters to Helen.

Reenie Ladies, can I have your attention please? That
            includes you, Miss Harper! I have a wee surprise.
            Correspondence from our star player south of the
            border!

*Reenie holds out the other letter and the parcel. Harry
snatches the letter and throws the parcel to Mo, who catches
it with ease.*

Harry   A letter fae Alice!

Lil   Read it out!

Harry   [*Reading*] 'Hello my friends,
            I hope this finds you well? I write from sunny
            Preston! Actually, we seldom see the sun, it rains
            constantly. And I thought Edinburgh was bad!'

Reenie Naewhere can be this bad!

Harry   [*Reading*] 'My landlady is a Mrs Neill, and her cooking is *awful*. Any food parcels will be *gratefully* received!'

Mo   Oh poor love. I'll send her some soup.

Daisy   Tae Preston?!

Mo   Dinnae worry, I'll let it go cold first.

Harry   [*Reading*] 'Work at Dick, Kerr's factory is fine. Different from making our beloved wellie boots, but a similar atmosphere. There are women from all over – Wales, Ireland, even some from the Caribbean. But I miss Edinburgh.'

Lil   We miss you Alice!

Harry   [*Reading*] 'The football team is just *wonderful*. The girls are a terrific bunch. Lily Parr is delightful company. She smokes like a chimney, and has a wicked sense of humour. She is also the *best* footballer I have ever seen. She took a penalty against a male professional goalkeeper. Afterwards, he said, and I quote: 'Get me to the hospital as quick as you can, she's gone and broken me flamin' arm!' Daisy, I remembered it was your birthday soon, so knitted a scarf in the colours we wear. Welcome to the family!'

Mo gives the parcel to Daisy. She unwraps a black and white scarf. Mo puts the scarf round Daisy's shoulders, giving her a wee hug. Daisy gives a little smile.

'All in all I have settled in well. Do write and let me know your news. Nothing would be nicer than to hear from you all. Love, Alice.'

Mo   Oh, that's just lovely. All she needs now is tae find hersel' a nice man.

Harry and Lil exchange a look and a giggle.

Harry Aye right!

Lil   We should all write back to her!

Mo   Aye, I'll send her a wee postcard or something.

Helen More good news! Dick, Kerr's Ladies are heading north for some matches in Scotland and they're proposing a rematch against us at Tynecastle! Alice is coming back!

Reenie Right ladies, it's knocking off time.

Helen Let's get training!

The Women leave, except Daisy and Helen, who watches Daisy from a distance. Daisy takes off her scarf and discards it before turning to leave. She stops and goes back for it before exiting.

SCENE NINE

The Ban

Helen On the eleventh hour, of the eleventh day, in the eleventh month in 1918, peace was declared. And the rest of our men were coming hame. Alice's brothers. Mo's wee boy, David. Daisy's Johnnie was already hame. Our men were never the same. But the factory was as busy as ever.

Mo, Lil, Harry, Daisy, and Reenie enter.

Morning girls!

Mo [*To the audience*] This is aboot six months later. Scene nine.

Lil Have you heard what the bloody government have done now? This Pre-War Practice thing?

Daisy Whit?

Reenie The Restoration of Pre-War Practices Act. It means returning servicemen are getting their pre-war jobs back.

Harry But what about us?

Lil Aye, we're good workers!

Reenie Doesnae matter. We all got jobs that the men left when they went tae fight. If enough men come back...

Soldier 1 and Soldier 2 appear.

Soldier 1 I'm looking for Miss Brown?

Reenie That's me.

Soldier 1 I'm starting back the day. I'm the supervisor.

Reenie Aye. Here's all you need tae know. I'll see ye at
training, girls.

Reenie leaves the space.

Whining Whingeing Women

Soldier 1 [*Singing*]
I am a soldier, hame from the front line,
Ye' kept my seat warm, but that profession's mine!
Dinnae disparage, or protest, or roar,
It's what I deserve for surviving the War!

[*Spoken*] Right then. There's gonnae be some
changes aroond here.

Harry Eh... dinnae think so pal!

Lil Aye! Ye cannae just come in here and start bossing
us around!

Soldier 1 & 2 [*Singing*]
We're both soldiers, hame from our tour,
Ye' kept making wellies, but those jobs are oors!
Dinnae disparage, or protest, or roar,
It's what we deserve for surviving the War!

Soldier 1 [*Spoken*] Maureen Jardine? Helen Matthews?
We're going to have tae let you go.

Mo No... please...

Helen Can I ask why?

Soldier 1 We've got mair men being demobbed. They're
entitled tae their jobs back.

Lil You cannae do this, it's no' fair!

Soldier 2 Dinnae talk tae us aboot fair! You women taking
oor jobs, that's no' fair!

Lil Well, we dinnae have tae put up wi' this! If they go,
we all go. Come on girls.

Mo and Helen exit, but Harry and Daisy stay where they are.

What are ye daein'?

Harry Sorry Lil. I cannae afford tae stop working.

Daisy Me neither. Johnnie needs me.

Lil I cannae afford it either. But I ken the difference
between right and wrong. [*Pause*] Suit yersel's.

Harry We've still got the team, Lil…

Lil exits. Man 2, Man 3 and Man 4 enter during the next verse.

Soldier 1 & 2 [*Singing*]
We're aw soldiers, hame from the Somme,

Man 2, Man 3 & Man 4
Verdun and Passchendaele, Contalmaison,
Dinnae disparage, or protest, or roar,
It's what men deserve for surviving the War!

Soldier 1 [*Spoken*] Daisy Robertson? Harriet Harper?

Harry Took ye's long enough eh.

Daisy But, I cannae stop, my husband…

Soldier 2 No' my problem hen. I dinnae make the rules.

Harry and Daisy exit.

All [*Singing*]
Whining whingeing women, won't you hear what
     we've tae say,
We wrung oor hands in German blood to bring you
     victory,
Our sacrifice, lest you forget, is etched in history,
We thank you all, but now we're hame, we don'twant
     Sweet FA.

*The **Soldiers** and **Men** leave the space, except for **Helen**, who becomes herself once more.*

Helen [*To the audience*] Our jobs were gone. So much for victory! We kept playing, along with a lot of the former factory teams. And the crowds kept growing, as did the amount of money we raised for charity. We were still doing our bit.

Daisy, Lil, Harry, Mo and Reenie enter in their strips, having just finished a game.

[*To Women*] Well done ladies, another impressive victory! Twenty-two games in a row is some record!

Daisy It was busy the day, eh?

Harry Ken! Must have been five thousand folk in the ground.

Reenie Mair like eight thousand!

Lil Somebody asked me tae sign an autograph!

Reenie As long as you didnae use 'Theda Bara'.

Lil   . . .

Reenie You didnae!

Mo   Now folk really will think she's playing!

Harry I got asked for a quote for the *Evening News*. The chancer didnae write doon what I said, then asked me how my husband feels aboot me playing!

Daisy He never did!

Harry Aye! He's lucky I didnae boot him in the...

Helen Thank you Harry!

Reenie I reckon you could write a better article than him, Harry.

Lil   Here, where was Big Mary the day?

Mo   She's no' well, hen. I'm taking her some soup round the night.

Daisy You and yer soup!

Mo   Well, I made a batch for ma laddie coming hame at the end o' the week, got plenty tae spare. It'll cheer her up an' all.

Reenie Mo, yer a saint!

Lil   Is she alright?

Mo   She's just got a wee cold.

Helen Better keep your distance, can't have you getting ill too!

Mo   Ach, dinnae worry aboot me, hen!

Reenie I ken a few folk who've got it tae, mind.

Helen   I heard the soldiers are bringing it back wi' them.

Mo   What are ye's like? For Heaven's sake, I'm only
         popping in for a cuppy, I'll stay oot her way. I'll see
         ye's at training!

Mo leaves the space. Helen addresses the audience.

Helen   That was the last time we saw Mo for a while.
         Turned out Mary had the Spanish Flu.

Reenie Mo caught it too. It was awful.

Lil   We couldn't go and see her, it was too risky.

Reenie Her poor laddie couldnae even see her when he got
         hame fae France.

Lil   Mo was a fighter though. She pulled through. But
         Mary...

Harry   She was all alone at the end.

Daisy   She tried to hold on for her husband coming hame
         fae France.

Reenie But she couldnae.

The Women exit, leaving Helen alone.

Helen   We started to hear stories of people getting sick in
         the morning and dying by nightfall. We were told to
         quarantine. Wear masks over our mouths. Can you
         imagine that? Our match against Dick, Kerr's was
         postponed. So we started to drift apart. The season

was curtailed and lots of teams were very unhappy. But not to worry, the game will be in safe hands until we return...

The SFA, with the exception of Campbell, enter the space, looking forlorn. They unenthusiastically hum their theme song.

Lord Scunthorpe Oh, come on chaps! Someone *MUST* be able to think of a way to stop wo...wo...

All [*Unenthusiastically*] Women's football.

Lord Scunthorpe The war ended three years...even the Spanish Flu couldn't stop them!

Abercrombie I heard there was a crowd of 53,000 at Everton's Goodison Park for a women's game!

Buchanan I heard they had to turn 15,000 people away!

Lord Dundee There were fewer people at the men's FA Cup final last year!

Secretary Watt Well, it seems the women's game is going from strength to strength...so it could be worth our while to let them keep playing?

All WHAT?

Campbell hurriedly enters in an excited state.

Campbell *The British Medical Journal*!

Abercrombie What are you blathering about, Campbell?

Campbell The medical profession called for a ban on the women's game in 1894.

Buchanan Ah, yes! We should have banned them back then!

Campbell A Dr Mary Scharlieb of Harley Street, a gynecol…lady doctor, called football the 'most unsuitable game, too much for a woman's physical frame'.

Buchanan But that was twenty-seven years ago!

Abercrombie We don't have a more current prognosis?

Lord Scunthorpe Yes, what's your point, Campbell?

Campbell I'm sure we could [*rubs his fingers and thumb together*] 'persuade' some eminent doctors to supply *new* evidence against?

Lord Scunthorpe Brilliant! Do we know any?

Buchanan It just so happens that my brother is in medicine.

All Is he?

Buchanan He's a surgeon.

All Is he?

Buchanan Well…he's a veterinary surgeon.

Lord Scunthorpe Close enough! See to it he writes us a favourable article of evidence.

Buchanan Of course. But, gentlemen, will it be enough to ban the strumpets?

Abercrombie Well…I want to know about the money! What are they doing with it all?

Secretary Watt All ticket monies raised are helping ex-servicemen and their charities. They're raising money for men…a higher percentage than men raise for men. In fact, men are under no obligation to put any monies towards charity, but women are legally bound...

Buchanan Profiting from charity?! Really?

Campbell Speaking of which, I've heard they are raising money for the striking coal miners.

Buchanan Bloody Bolsheviks!

Campbell The suffrage movement has been very vocal...

Abercrombie Giving them the vote was a huge mistake...

Buchanan We must stop them playing!

All Ban them!

Lord Scunthorpe Restrict their options! Let's instruct the Association clubs to withdraw the use of their pitches.

Campbell And, prevent any of our bloody members acting as referees or linesmen for their games.

Lord Scunthorpe Gentlemen, we have our resolution. Anything else to add, Watt?

Silence as they all look at Secretary Watt.

Abercrombie Damn it man, answer him!

Secretary Watt [*Browbeaten*] I have nothing... Sir.

Lord Scunthorpe Bravo! All those in favour?

Each member raises his voting paddle to show 'AYE'.

Lord Scunthorpe Hmm, good show, Dundee!

Lord Dundee   I'm learning! And thank you for buying me a
new vote thing!

*Lord Dundee turns his paddle round, to reveal it has 'AYE'
written on both sides.*

Shan't get confused now!

Lord Scunthorpe   Resolution is hereby adopted. This,
gentlemen, will finally kill off the women's game.

All   Huzzah!

Lord Scunthorpe   Bravo Watt. Hand me the resolution,
would you?

*Secretary Watt does so, and through the following speech,
the SFA transform back into the Women.*

Reenie   Official resolution of fifth of December, 1921 from
the FA. [*Reading*] 'Council felt impelled to express
the strong opinion that the game of football is quite
unsuitable for females and should not be encouraged.
The Council are further of the opinion that an
excessive proportion of the receipts are absorbed in
expenses and an inadequate percentage devoted to
charitable objects. For these reasons the Council
requests the Clubs belonging to the Association
refuse the use of their grounds for such matches.'

Daisy   Really?

*Lil and Reenie start to sing. During this, the Women take off
their boots and hold them up at the end of the song.*

Hang Up Our Boots

Lil/Reenie
> *We toiled on the work line to help fight the Hun,*
> *While the boys on the front line had nowhere to run,*
> *We ran on the football fields, playing our game,*
> *They marched into battle fields, never the same.*

All
> *We did our bit, we made our choice,*
> *Picked up the slack and discovered our voice,*
> *Now down to dogma from blazers and suits,*
> *It's time for us women to hang up our boots.*
>
> *We welcomed them home with our arms open wide,*
> *Their stiff upper lips hiding anguish inside,*
> *We gave up our jobs and they took the ball hame,*
> *Don't try to tell us it's only a game.*
>
> *We did our bit, we made our choice,*
> *Picked up the slack and discovered our voice,*
> *Now down to dogma from blazers and suits,*
> *It's time for us women to hang up our boots.*

Helen That's how the footballing authorities saw it going. We saw it differently...

Daisy Stop playing? Nut...I'm no' daein that!

Reenie Ken, no' bloody likely!

Lil I know where they can shove their ban!

Harry Aye! Right up their...

Helen Thank you, Harry! We arranged one last match at Tynecastle Park to be played before the ban took effect. A derby game against our local rivals Ramage & Ferguson's seemed appropriate. They were just as riled up as us. And we'd be damned if the blazers were going to put us down!

The Women exit.

SCENE TEN

The Reunion

Daisy enters the space.

Daisy Alright gaffer. [*Looking around*] Where's everyone else?

Helen They'll be along. I wanted you here earlier.

Daisy You don't have to worry about me, I'll no' complain to the ref, even if he's at it.

Helen Today's referee is Bobby Walker. I can assure you he won't be 'at it'.

Daisy You're kidding! He's a Hearts legend!

Helen He's been very supportive of the women's game.

Daisy Well, I absolutely promise I'll no' complain the day!

Helen Promise? No complaints?

Daisy Promise, gaffer.

Alice enters, holding a letter in her hand.

Daisy ...

Helen You promised you wouldn't complain, Miss Robertson.

Helen leaves the space, smiling.

Daisy What are you doing here?

Alice   I'm playing today.

Daisy   You look different.

Alice   Do I? How?

Daisy   Dae ken. Happy I suppose.

Alice   This is for you.

Alice hands Daisy the letter.

>   Don't open it yet. There are some things I need to
>   say first.

Daisy   Oh?

Alice   You changed my life the day I met you. You and
football. If it wasn't for that day, I wouldn't be where
I am now. I wanted to say thank you.

Daisy   Nae bother.

Beat

Alice   And I'm sorry about how I left. When you said you
didn't care for me, I got so angry. But I want you to
know that I do still care.

Daisy   How long you back for? Are you staying with your
old man?

Alice   I'm leaving after the game. The family bridges are
well and truly burned. My brothers were furious that
I left, even after all I did for father. I tried to make
peace with them, but...

Silence

I hope you accept my apology. And I hope Johnnie realises how lucky he is.

Daisy   Alice, I...I left Johnnie.

Beat

Alice   You left him? When?

Daisy   A while ago now.

Alice   Oh Daisy...Why? What happened?

Daisy   He got so low. And angry. I tried tae help, cos that's what ye dae when ye love someone, but...then I realised I didnae love him. His mum takes better care of him than I ever could anyway. Folk turned their back on me. For breaking my vows. For not doing my duty. For being cowardly.

Alice   I think you're courageous.

Daisy   So now ye' know.

Alice   Is there anything else you want to tell me?

Daisy   Alice, I...I dunno what to say...

Alice   Try.

Daisy   I'm scared of how I feel about you! Terrified. It's like I don't know who I am anymore.

Alice   How do you feel about me? Just tell me the truth!

Daisy suddenly kisses Alice.

Daisy   The truth is I think I'm in love with you and I cannae cope wi it.

Alice   You think you're in love with me?

Daisy   Aye! But how could we even be together? I couldnae hold yer hand walking down Princes Street, I couldnae just kiss you whenever I felt like it...

Alice   You just did.

Daisy   You're no' helping.

They are interrupted by the rest of the Women, who rush over to greet Alice. Daisy busies herself getting ready for the game.

Mo   Alice! So good tae have you back!

Reenie   You look great, hen!

Harry   Aye! Sunny Preston must be agreeing wi' you!

Lil   You alright Daisy?

Daisy   I'm fine.

Reenie   [*To Alice*] Are ye still loving it doon there?

Alice   Yes, it's wonderful!

Lil   What aboot the ban?

Alice   It's not stopping us. We'll play wherever we can! Dick, Kerr's are going to the United States.

Mo   America?

Alice   Yes. On a tour. Canada too. Then we're setting up a separate league. The English Ladies Football Association. Over 150 clubs so far. Anyway, enough about me, what about you lot?

Lil   Well, the suffrage campaign is keeping me busy.

Harry And she's my new housemate.

Lil   Christ, I thought my Jack was clarty...

Harry Aye, aye... It's because I'm so busy wi' my new job. I write aboot the football for the paper. Harry Harper, *Edinburgh Evening News*. Pleased tae meet ye'!

Alice Pull the other one!

Mo   It's true.

Alice You're using a pseudonym!

Harry Technically, no. I am Harry Harper. But I get one of Reenie's lads fae the factory to hand the reports in for me. Costs me a pack o' Woodbines, but I've taken that much chocolate off him over the years, it only seems fair.

Alice You're back at the factory?

Reenie Aye! No' as a supervisor, but a bookkeeper.

Lil   The first woman they've ever had daein' it!

Alice Good for you! Mo?

Mo   I'm labelling bottles at the brewery. My laddie's working there too. It's nice no tae be rattling around an empty hoose again!

Alice How's he doing?

Mo   He's clarty as ever. His soup-making's coming on though.

Alice   You're going to keep the team going though, aren't you?

Silence

Helen   Ach, I'm getting a bit old for all this. It's a young woman's game.

Mo   Aye, what with work and ma laddie being hame...

Harry   I'm enjoying writing about it mair than playin'...

Reenie   It was fun while it lasted eh?

Lil   I cannae believe I'm hearing this! Well, I'm no' stopping. I'll start a new team. We'll kick a can down Gorgie Road if we have to.

Mo   They'll no' let ye', hen.

Lil   I've got tae try. This cannae be it. Our fight is just beginning.

Helen   You will continue the fight for us.

Mo   Aye. Good for you hen.

Reenie   It's getting noisy oot there eh?

Harry   Aye! It sounds busier than usual.

Reenie   I'm a wee bit nervous.

Mo   I've got just the thing. It was meant to be for after.

Harry   Please tell me it's no' soup...

Mo pulls a bottle of King George IV whisky from her bag and hands it to Reenie.

Mo   It was supposed tae be for after!

Reenie Thanks hen. Can I just say something. I didnae know you all before we started playing football. I've never been more pleased that I took up this ludicrous endeavour. It's been a hell o' a journey. And even though we'll no' be playing after today, we'll be team mates for life. Tae fitbaw and friends!

All   Fitbaw and friends!

Daisy has opened the letter. She's in shock.

Daisy [*To Alice*] Is this a joke?

Alice No.

Harry What is it?

The rest have stopped what they're doing, intrigued.

Daisy It's a letter.

Mo   Whit's happening?

Lil   Daisy's got a letter.

Mo   I can see that! Well, who's it fae?

Daisy It's from Alfred Frankland.

Helen The Dick, Kerr's Ladies manager.

Daisy He's saying his offer of a place is still open.

Lil   That's brilliant!

Reenie You lucky thing!

Alice He remembers you. When I told him I was coming back, he asked me to pass the letter on to you.

Daisy stares at the letter. The Women look at her until Harry can't take it anymore.

Harry Well?

Daisy Well what?

Lil Are ye' going to Preston?

Harry Tae America?

Daisy can't speak.

Alice Well?

Helen blows her whistle.

Helen Ladies, it's almost time for kick-off. Heads in the game!

Harry/Mo But we need to know!

Helen Save personal matters till afterwards. I have it on good authority that we have 15,000 supporters to entertain.

Mo 15,000? Where's that bottle?

Harry Bloody hell!

Lil Right, mind if that ootside left is playing again, we need tae watch her.

Harry Aye. Oh Alice, look out for goalposts eh!

Alice Very funny!

Lil   And you watch the offside trap, Daisy, we ken how worked up ye' get.

Harry   Mind that first training game?

Daisy   For the last time, I...

All   Wisnae offside!

Helen   Right ladies, here we go. One last game!

Alice   Shall we?

All   Come on the NBR!

The Women become Men at the game.

Ann   What the hell's that NBR? You're just sitting back watching them! Alice McEwan - what's she playing at?

Harry   Great ball! Well played.

Lil   There she is! Get it oot wide!

Mo   Make a run fer her, ya daftie!

Helen   Get yer heid oan it!

Mo   Glad we still have Lil McKenzie. She drives the team forward.

Reenie   Can't believe they're playing Robertson again. She's bobbins.

Harry   [*Agreeing*] Bobbins.

NBR score - the crowd roars.

Alice   Yaaaass! Daisy Robertson! Always believed in you!

With that, the Men become the Women again and they start to sing.

Yours Till You Die (Reprise)

All   [*Singing*]
The crowds are singing, our ears are ringing
Shouting our name as we're playing the game,
Scarves raised, voices in praise
Can't move nor think nor breathe nor blink
And as we appear, the crowd starts to thrive –
We've never felt anything so raw and alive.

'Yours till you die, yours till you die!'
From the stadium up ahead comes the cry.
'Yours till you die, yours till you die!'
Now my heart knows the reason why.

EPILOGUE

Helen   Daisy was lucky.

Reenie She had a choice.

Mo   An opportunity to decide.

Lil   But for most women, freedom of choice was still a
            fight.

Helen   The ban on the women's game remained in place for
            fifty years!

Rosie   In 1971, UEFA's members voted 31-1 in favour of
            formally recognising the women's game.

Reenie Guess who was the one and only nation to vote
            against this?

Alice   Scotland!

Daisy   It took another three years for the Scottish Football
            Association to formally lift the ban here.

Harry   Heid the baws!

Reenie Just imagine where the women's game would be
            now if there was no ban!

Lil   We've still come a long way since then.

Ann   Rose Reilly, a young woman from Stewarton in
            Ayrshire, was so good, she became the only
            Scottish person to win a World Cup when she
            represented Italy in 1984.

Alice   She was some player.

Mo   Back here, in 2019, Scotland's Women qualified for the World Cup!

Harry   The first time a Scottish team had qualified in twenty years.

Alice   The same year, Hearts Women won promotion to the SWPL 1.

Lil   And Hearts remain the only top flight team in Scotland to have a female chair.

Helen   The women's game is going from strength to strength nowadays.

Daisy   But that's a story for another time!

All   This is our story!

Winning Working Women (Reprise)

All   [*Singing*]
Winning working women won't you hear what we've
*   tae say,*
We ran oursel's intae the ground tae win the right
*   tae play,*
We've shown the world we're no' too frail to step
*   intae the fray,*
And if you try tae take it back, we'll give you…
We'll give you…
We'll give you…
Sweet FA!

The End.

TIPPERMUIR BOOKS

Tippermuir Books Ltd is an independent publishing company based in Perth, Scotland.

Publishing History

Spanish Thermopylae (2009)

Battleground Perthshire (2009)

Perth: Street by Street (2012)

Born in Perthshire (2012)

In Spain with Orwell (2013)

Trust (2014)

Perth: As Others Saw Us (2014)

Love All (2015)

A Chocolate Soldier (2016)

The Early Photographers of Perthshire (2016)

Taking Detective Novels Seriously: The Collected Crime Reviews of Dorothy L Sayers (2017)

Walking with Ghosts (2017)

No Fair City: Dark Tales from Perth's Past (2017)

The Tale o the Wee Mowdie that wantit tae ken wha keeched on his heid (2017)
Shortlisted for Scots Children's Book of the Year 2019

Hunters: Wee Stories from the Crescent: A Reminiscence of Perth's Hunter Crescent (2017)

A Little Book of Carol's (2018)

Flipstones (2018)

Perth: Scott's Fair City: The Fair Maid of Perth & Sir Walter Scott – A Celebration & Guided Tour (2018)

God, Hitler, and Lord Peter Wimsey: Selected Essays, Speeches and Articles by Dorothy L Sayers (2019)

Perth & Kinross: A Pocket Miscellany: A Companion for Visitors and Residents (2019)

The Piper of Tobruk: Pipe Major Robert Roy, MBE, DCM (2019)

The 'Gig Docter o Athole': Dr William Irvine & The Irvine Memorial Hospital (2019)

Afore the Highlands: The Jacobites in Perth, 1715-16 (2019)

'Where Sky and Summit Meet': Flight Over Perthshire – A History: Tales of Pilots, Airfields, Aeronautical Feats, & War (2019)

Diverted Traffic (2020)

Authentic Democracy: An Ethical Justification of Anarchism (2020)

'If Rivers Could Sing': A Scottish River Wildlife Journey. A Year in the Life of the River Devon as it flows through the Counties of Perthshire, Kinross-shire & Clackmannanshire (2020)
Shortlisted Scotland's National Book Awards 2021, 'New Book' (Saltire Literary Awards).

A Squatter o Bairnrhymes (2020)
by Stuart A Paterson, Scots Writer of the Year 2020

In a Sma Room Songbook: From the Poems by William Soutar (2020)

The Nicht Afore Christmas: the much-loved yuletide tale in Scots (2020)
Shortlisted for Scots Children's Book of the Year 2021

Ice Cold Blood (David Millar, 2021)

The Black Watch and the Great War
(Derek Patrick and Fraser Brown (editors), 2021)

The Perth Riverside Nursery & Beyond:
A Spirit of Enterprise and Improvement
(Elspeth Bruce and Pat Kerr, 2021)

Beyond the Swelkie: A Collection of Poems & Writings to Mark the Centenary of George Mackay Brown (1921-1996)
(Jim Mackintosh and Paul S Philippou (editors), 2021)

Dying to Live: The Remarkable True Story of Scotland's Sickest Survivor of Covid-19
(Grant and Amanda Macintyre, 2021)

The Shanter Legacy: The Search for the Grey Mare's Tail
(Garry Stewart, 2021)

Fatal Duty: Scotland's Cop Killers, Killer Cops & More... from 1812 to 1952 (Gary Knight, 2021)

Forthcoming

A Scottish Wildlife Odyssey: In Search of Scotland's Wild Secrets (Keith Broomfield, 2022)

A War of Two Halves
(Tim Barrow, Paul Beeson and Bruce Strachan)

William Soutar: Collected Poetry, Volume I
(Kirsteen McCue and Paul S Philippou (editors), 2022)

William Soutar: Collected Poetry, Volume II
(Kirsteen McCue and Paul S Philippou (editors), 2023)

Berries Fae Banes: An owersettin in Scots o the poems bi Pino Mereu scrievit in tribute tae Hamish Henderson
(Jim Macintosh, 2022)

Perthshire 101: A Poetic Gazetteer of the Big County
(Andy Jackson (editor), 2022)

Perth City Activity Book: Exploring the Past and Present
(Felicity Graham, 2022)

All Tippermuir Books titles are available from bookshops and online booksellers. They can also be purchased directly (with free postage & packing (UK only) - minimum charges for overseas delivery) from **www.tippermuirbooks.co.uk.**

Tippermuir Books Ltd can be contacted at **mail@tippermuirbooks.co.uk.**

TIPPERMUIR
BOOKS LIMITED